Foreverism

Theory Redux
Series editor: Laurent de Sutter

Published Titles

Mark Alizart, *Cryptocommunism*

Armen Avanessian, *Future Metaphysics*

Franco Berardi, *The Second Coming*

Alfie Bown, *The Playstation Dreamworld*

Laurent de Sutter, *Narcocapitalism*

Diedrich Diederichsen, *Aesthetics of Pop Music*

Roberto Esposito, *Persons and Things*

Boris Groys, *Becoming an Artwork*

Graham Harman, *Immaterialism*

Helen Hester, *Xenofeminism*

Srećko Horvat, *The Radicality of Love*

Lorenzo Marsili, *Planetary Politics*

Dominic Pettman, *Infinite Distraction*

Eloy Fernández Porta, *Nomography*

Mikkel Bolt Rasmussen, *Late Capitalist Fascism*

Nick Srnicek, *Platform Capitalism*

Grafton Tanner, *Foreverism*

Oxana Timofeeva, *Solar Politics*

Foreverism

Grafton Tanner

polity

First published in 2023 by Polity Press

Polity Press
65 Bridge Street
Cambridge CB2 1UR, UK

Polity Press
111 River Street
Hoboken, NJ 07030, USA

ISBN-13: 978-1-5095-5805-6
ISBN-13: 978-1-5095-5806-3(pb)

A catalogue record for this book is available from the British Library.

Library of Congress Catalog Number: 2023931487

Typeset in 12.5 on 15pt Adobe Garamond
by Cheshire Typesetting Ltd, Cuddington, Cheshire
Printed and bound in Great Britain by CPI Group (UK) Ltd, Croydon

For further information on Polity, visit our website:
politybooks.com

Contents

For Anna

Acknowledgments

First thanks goes to Laurent de Sutter, who sent a bottle into the sea asking if I'd be interested in writing a short theoretical intervention into the contemporary. He was kind enough to indulge my ideas and allow me the freedom to explore. My gratitude extends to John Thompson, Lindsey Wimpenny, and the entire team at Polity for shepherding this book to publication, and to Oriol Rosell for kickstarting it all.

Early drafts of these ideas were presented at Queens College in 2021 and for the Nostalgia Movements Conference in Zagreb in 2022. Thank you to Josh Chapdelaine and Dario Vuger for inviting me to speak.

ACKNOWLEDGMENTS

My family has supported me from the beginning, and I'm forever thankful for them. Anna is my advocate, my peace. My love for her will last forever, of that I'm sure.

When Nothing Ever Ends

Section 17 of Hans Gross's 1911 book *Criminal Psychology* concerns "the question of home-sickness," which, he points out, "is of essential significance and must not be undervalued" when studying the criminal mind. He maintains that if nostalgia cannot be relieved, it can fester in a person and make them murderous:

> So then, if the home-sick person is able, he tries to destroy his nostalgia through the noisiest and most exciting pleasures; if he is not, he sets fire to a house or in case of need, kills somebody—in short what he needs is explosive relief. Such events are so numerous that they ought to have considerable attention.[1]

The early twentieth century produced a plethora of opinions on the *nostalgia reaction*, and Hans Gross was not the only positivist to link the emotion with criminality. Karl Jaspers contributed his own assumptions in his 1909 dissertation, writing about a young maidservant in 1795 who moved away from home to pursue work but eventually burned down her place of employment because she was homesick.[2] In a 1922 study, psychiatrist Maximilian Bresowsky told the story of a maid who murdered her four-year-old charge because killing the child was the only way she could leave work and return home.[3] Ernst Kretschmer, the German psychiatrist who developed a classification system matching body types with personality traits, also made the connection in 1934:

> The nostalgia-reaction in the form of arson and child-murder is a typical syndrome in maidservants between the ages of fourteen and seventeen. The girls who exhibit it are usually infantile and weakly, with retarded pubescence. . . . In this lamb-like, timid, and autistic way, such girls often exhibit schizoid features.[4]

Psychologist Edmund Smith Conklin will claim as late as 1935 that "the homesick reaction" can result in "explosive, or uncontrollable, criminal actions, arson, and even murder." But he will surmise that nostalgia is declining thanks to "the greater amount of travel and shifting of places of residence occurring in modern civilization." To prevent nostalgia from occurring, he will caution parents against excessive "petting and coddling which develops parental fixations."[5]

By the early twentieth century, nostalgia's threat was its power to turn an ordinary, agentic individual into a criminal. To the positivists, however, this came as no surprise. In his literature review of nostalgia, Willis H. McCann cites psychologist Karl Marbe, who "did not think it strange that homesickness sometimes would cause crime. He explained that those who can relieve themselves of homesickness by committing a crime will do so unless restrained."[6]

Earlier writings discussed the possibility that individuals from rural areas might be particularly vulnerable to nostalgia. On February 10, 1864, Assistant Surgeon of the US Army J. Theodore Calhoun presented a paper entitled "Nostalgia as a Disease of Field Service." He argued that troops were dangerously at risk of contracting the disease and that it sometimes caused other diseases to spread, leading him to label nostalgia "a complication to be dreaded as one of the most serious that could befall the patient." Calhoun said that soldiers from rural backgrounds were more susceptible to nostalgia because "a country boy is more at home." The soldier from the city, on the other hand, is stronger and more mature; he "cares not where he is, or where he eats, while his country cousin, pines for the old homestead and his father's groaning board." But it was on the battlefield, Calhoun declared, where rural men could really prove their manhood and thus cure their nostalgia:

Any influence that will tend to render the patient more manly, will exercise a curative power. In boarding schools, as perhaps many of us will remember, ridicule is wholly relied upon, and will often be found effective in camp. Unless the disease affects a number of the same organization ... the patient can often be laughed out of it by his comrades, or reasoned out of it by appeals to his manhood; but of all potent agents, an active campaign, with its attendant marches, and more particularly its battles, is the best curative.[7]

The talk was popular. *The Medical and Surgical Reporter* published it two weeks later, and excerpts appeared in *Scientific American* that April, under the title "Home-sickness as a Malady." The Medical Society hosted a discussion on nostalgia with other army physicians. Some noted that a lack of cleanliness was the first symptom of nostalgia. Others doubled down on the supposition that soldiers from too "domestic" a background, who haven't "'roughed it' before," were prone to contracting the disease.[8]

Following Calhoun's logic, psychologist L. W. Kline believed that educated travelers were too intellectual to be bothered by nostalgic emotions. The mature, civilized subject could embark on adventure without feeling an unhealthy attachment to home. They embraced the future, while the "lover of home" was stuck in the past. Kline ended his 1898 paper on nostalgia with these words:

The migrant is cosmopolitan, has manifold interests, and finds profitable objects and kindred spirits in a variety of situations. He may be found in the commercial, speculative, daring, progressive, macroscopic interests of the world. The lover of home is provincial, plodding and timid. He is the world's hod-carrier. His interests are identified with the conservative and microscopic affairs of society.[9]

The positivist discourses on nostalgia might seem extreme to us now. But because nostalgia has an uncanny ability to wrench people out of the present, it posed a threat to the civilizing process promoted by juridico-medical positivists. They thought that escaping from the present through nostalgic reflection or homesick yearning might cause a person to be backward and unable to work. Many of their writings were inflected with racist, sexist, and nationalistic sentiments. In praise of the almighty present, the medicalization of nostalgia allowed for deeply rooted prejudices to be reaffirmed.

Antinostalgic positivists were the authors of a new genre of writing linking the figure of abnormality with nostalgia, thus producing the idea of the nostalgic subject. A nostalgic subject became, in the words of Foucault, an "individual to be corrected": the one who is "regular in his irregularity" and "appears to require correction because all the usual techniques, procedures, and attempts at training ... have failed to correct him." Nonconforming individuals, those who failed to adopt the identity of the progressive man of the Enlightenment, were routinely accused of backwardness. The early twentieth century witnessed this emergence of the modern nostalgic subject, the longing, yearning individual in need of "supercorrection."[10]

Over the course of the twentieth century a massive shift will occur. The opinions on nostalgia will be rearranged. Less than a hundred years after Bresowsky, Kretschmer, and Conklin linked nostalgia with criminality, Fabrik Brands, an ad agency out of London, compiled a list of tips for companies to conduct successful nostalgia marketing campaigns:

1. *Know your inspiration.* If you want to use retro ideas effectively in your new campaign, then you need to ask yourself . . . How can you make nostalgia work well for your current campaign, and what features will you need to think about to ensure that you get the attention of your audience?

2. *Keep your audience and personality in mind.* Before you can engage in a powerful nostalgia marketing strategy, you need to make sure that you're drawing images and ideas from the right generation, to appease the right demographic.

3. *Pair nostalgia with social media.* If nostalgia is the bait for your marketing campaign, then social media is the fishing rod . . . People don't just want to enjoy the memories of a nostalgic image or sound, they want to be able to link their friends and family members to the experience and say "Hey, remember this?"

4. *Tap into brand history (if you can).* If your company has already been around for some time, then a great way to increase the impact of your nostalgia marketing strategy, is to tap into some powerful brand history.

5. *Pay close attention to detail.* Finally, when it comes to nostalgia marketing . . . it's generally a good idea to combine retro concepts with new ideas to make the experience more engaging and exciting for your customers.[11]

What happened to nostalgia? How did it go from a condition of abnormality, even criminality, in the early twentieth century to a marketing tactic today? We obviously don't think nostalgia can cause a person to commit murder anymore, or advertising firms wouldn't encourage companies to use nostalgia in their marketing. The truth is, there actually isn't much of a difference between the words of the positivists and Fabrik Brands. In fact, they're both trying to accomplish the same thing: the eradication of longing.

Nostalgia After the Death of Progress

At first glance, it appears the history of nostalgia is a palatable progress narrative: over time physicians learned it wouldn't cause anyone to commit crime, and so now it has become a commodity flashing across screens, something anyone can feel and consume. For a long time, we comforted ourselves with this fable because it served as a metric by which we measured scientific advancement and medical enlightenment, evidence of our victory over other "outdated" conditions (vapors, hysteria) that, in hindsight, were human emotions pathologized and subjected to a disciplinary regime. At times it fooled us with the assumption that conditions in the past were more intense, deadlier, and that the achievements of science have tamed their wild tempests, placing them under control. We were certain that as the large mammals roaming the past have gone extinct, so too have the raging passions that were once so ungovernable they could kill. Either myth — that we advanced enough to learn nostalgia isn't a disease, or that progress refined its once unruly destruction — soothed any concern that traces of backwardness survived the march of progress.

The fable was so easy to tell. Nostalgia had its own origin story: the word first appeared in a 1688 dissertation by a nineteen-year-old medical student named Johannes Hofer. Conceived as a disease, nostalgia was then studied by numerous physicians through the eighteenth, nineteenth, and twentieth centuries. Most of them were looking for the cure to stop what they saw as a debilitating disease.

The discursive production of the nostalgic subject took its cues from neighboring pseudo-scientific theories of the time, including *atavism*, or the assumption that older, more primitive traits could reappear in certain groups of people. A popular strain of social Darwinism, atavism justified discussions of eugenics in order to "breed" out the throwback genes. Nostalgia became a weapon against minority populations accused of such backwardness.

But then, around the middle of the twentieth century, nostalgia was de-medicalized and quickly commodified. After the massive success of George Lucas's 1973 film *American Graffiti*, the marketing world started paying attention to nostalgia. In 1975, professor of marketing Donald W. Hendon wrote an op-ed in *Marketing News* arguing that the product life cycle — in which a product is introduced into the marketplace, grows, matures, saturates the market, and then declines — should be updated to account for a new trend, where product sales increase after they decline. He called this the "nostalgia tail" and attributed its development partly to the popularity of Broadway musicals like *Grease*, television programs like *Happy Days*, "and the Bicentennial market boom." Nostalgia wasn't a passing fad, Hendon claimed, and the marketing world needed to take it seriously.[12]

That same year psychologist George Rosen published an article questioning whether nostalgia had become a "forgotten" disorder of the mind. He argued that nostalgia hadn't disappeared but was spreading "under other labels" as the "psychological disabilities manifested by refugees, displaced persons, prisoners of war, and survivors of concentration camps," all of which "testify once again to man's inhumanity to man."[13] Freed from its positivist prison, nostalgia could drift under other guises to commodified destinations, while its medical associations were born again as other pathologies.

The popular culture of the time, however, was split on the matter. The American public received mixed signals in the 1970s and 1980s, as families tuned in to *Happy Days* and *The Wonder Years* while singer Don Henley implored: "Don't look back / You can never look back." In an episode of *The Mary Tyler Moore Show* from 1974, Lou Grant, played with a tough-guy demeanor by Ed Asner, tells the news team that he wants to do a "fresh" location feature for their station, WJM — "not something that's been done *over* and *over*." Mary suggests they do "a nostalgia piece" on the music and fashion of the mid-1960s, to highlight "how dumb and funny things are when you look back at them." She then reminisces about a teenage crush, and the men in the room roll their eyes. "I *hate* nostalgia," Lou grumbles. "I didn't like it then, and I don't like it now."[14]

Whereas positivist discourses targeted nostalgia as a disease to be cured, corporations eventually framed it as a consumable product, and advertisers would eventually discover just how lucrative nostalgia can be as a commodity — because consumers can theoretically satisfy their longing for the past through consumption. By framing the past as worth longing for, corporate capitalism could promise a return to the past through its products. It was a new twist on a tried-and-true capitalist formula: the marketing of a solution to a problem artificially amplified.

The commodification of nostalgia didn't quiet everyone's fears about the emotion's disorderly potential, but the punitive measures to defeat it were disappearing. What could a person threatened by nostalgia do? It was still necessary to tame this emergent figure, the modern nostalgic subject, but the methods to do so changed with the times. Gentle refinements in punishment became even more virtual. The calls to remain vigilant when criminals act, because their motive could be nostalgic, were slowly quieted. Corrective measures were replaced by therapeutic modalities, and these became increasingly moderated by the market. Experiencing and expressing nostalgia meant consuming it through television, cinema, music, and popular culture.

Meanwhile, the faith in progress was being tested. This was a problem because, for a long time, nostalgia was the conceptual foil to progress, its nemesis. Progress was the one weapon guaranteed to destroy every last homesick feeling, and evangelizers of progress were quick to claim that if a person focused too much on the past, they would be left behind. Only through the civilizing process, so it was thought, would people be saved from backwardness, a sentiment captured best in a French medical journal from the 1850s:

Happily, nostalgia diminishes day by day; by descending little by little among the masses, instruction will develop the intelligence of people, making them more and more capable of struggling against this disease. Everything that touches civilization, in perfecting the human species, makes man understand his role as an individual, his part in the common work, and, in enlightening his spirit, submits the impulses of his heart to reason.[15]

This old sentiment was echoed at the tenth Democratic presidential primary debate in

February 2020, when former South Bend, Indiana, mayor Pete Buttigieg accused Senator Bernie Sanders of nostalgia, thus associating him with Donald Trump and his nostalgically inflected political platform:

> The only way we're going to restore American credibility . . . is to actually win the presidency, and I am not looking forward to a scenario where it comes down to Donald Trump with his nostalgia for the social order of the 1950s and Bernie Sanders with a nostalgia for the revolutionary politics of the 1960s. This is not about what coups were happening in the 1970s or '80s, this is about the future. This is about 2020.[16]

The progress narratives of the 1850s did not have the same ring in 2020. (Buttigieg dropped out of the presidential race a few days after the debate.) They could not quiet the stormy worries of individuals who suspected that only the past can guarantee security and freedom in a world speeding towards collapse. Things are constantly shifting, changing, in flux. Everything seems so fragile, fleeting, and the only thing more horrifying than the shock of the present is the future, with its unknown atrocities waiting up the road ahead. So when appeals are made to progress, they are often scoffed at. Few would endorse the notion that things could get better. But there are still ham-fisted attempts to revive the dead corpse of progress. Tech corporations rhetorically weave their inventions into the narrative of progress and historicize them as the next great leap forward, whether they're driverless cars, digital currencies, or virtual reality platforms. It is hard to take them seriously. Only the most delusional technocrats would ever believe that the invention of the electric vehicle triggered a paradigm shift as transformative as the invention of the incandescent light bulb.

Since progress aged poorly into an unreliable myth, something was needed to solve the nostalgia reaction, something coeval with the exigencies of a therapeutic society, a cure masquerading as symptom. If progress wouldn't suffice, there needed to be another way to keep nostalgia at bay, one that wouldn't leave the past behind but that also refused to embrace the future. Instead, it would reboot the past. It would promise to eliminate the possibility of loss by keeping the past alive in the present, and as a result, nostalgia would finally be conquered.

Foreverism

Because nostalgia shapes a great deal of our culture and politics today, the usual move is to accuse our culture — producers and consumers alike — of being stuck in the past, of being too nostalgic, but if nostalgia is the emotion experienced when something normally absent becomes momentarily present, in our minds or in everyday life, then the constant presence of the past in the contemporary doesn't amount to "nostalgia" as much as something else.

I'm calling this discourse of keeping the past present *foreverism*. Foreverism gives people everywhere the notion that ours is a past-gazing society; to accept this as truth is to see only one side of the coin: foreverism's purpose is to eliminate nostalgia, just like yesterday's juridico-medical discourses. It does this sneakily, through the illusion of consumption and choice. Foreverism can trick us into regarding the present-day explosion of nostalgic content as proof of our longing for the past, but just because we have near-endless access to nostalgic content doesn't necessarily mean we are nostalgic. Maybe, in a world of retromaniacal plenty, when we have more access to the past than ever before, we haven't felt nostalgia in ages.

The discourse of foreverism sanctions a process I'll call *foreverizing*. Expanding cinematic "universes," cloud archiving, and even voice cloning technologies are all in the business of foreverizing, that is, of revitalizing things that have degraded, failed, or disappeared so they can remain active in the present forever. To foreverize something is not merely to preserve or restore it but to reanimate it in the present and ensure its future survival, forever. It is the rejuvenation or rebooting of things lost, the breathing of new life into moldering corpses. Rebooting older films, reviving bygone fashion trends, digitizing "memories": these developments prevent the old and (out)dated from disappearing into the past, *so that we won't miss them anymore* . . . so that we won't feel the pain of longing for the past — in other words, so that we won't feel nostalgic for it.

We have not arrived at a relaxed acceptance of nostalgia, nor have we tamed any nostalgic intensities once raging. The West is as anxious about nostalgia today as it was in the past, when medical professionals endeavored to find a cure for it. We have, instead, found new weapons for eradicating it. These weapons do not register as coercive, intrusive, or disciplinary, but they are covert and just as antinostalgic as the medical and punitive discourses that impugned nostalgia for centuries.

I have chosen the terms *foreverism* and *foreverizing* intentionally. I first encountered the word *foreverizing* on the website for iMemories, a digital transfer company. "At iMemories, we understand how important your memories are to you and your family," the "About Us" section states. "That's why we don't just digitize your old videos, movie films and photos to be playable now — we foreverize your memories to be relived over and over again."[17] This intrigued me. Why would the company, or its customers, associate the digital with the forever? That is, with permanence, accessibility, and organization? Because iMemories chose to use that term to distinguish itself from other companies that merely digitize analog "memories," it makes a claim about human memory that's become quite popular in the digital age, namely, that the digital ensures the security and playability of recorded memories that are otherwise difficult to ensure.

Shortly after that, I came across the term *foreverism* in the most unlikely of places: a marketing publication. In 2009 consumer trend firm TrendWatching issued a briefing titled "Foreverism: Consumers and businesses embracing conversations, lifestyles and products that are 'never done'." It argued that the "forever" should be as meaningful a concept for the marketing world as the "now" and outlined three characteristics of foreverism for businesses to consider: forever presence, forever beta, and forever conversing. The publication pointed out that the now hadn't disappeared, but the forever looked increasingly appealing. "Let's face it: many things *are* inherently transient and short-lived, and consumers like it that way," the briefing noted. "And in the looooong run, *nothing* lasts forever. But FOREVERISM and NOWISM aren't mutually exclusive. The opportunity lies in figuring out which processes, services, products currently are ephemeral when consumers would perhaps prefer some sort of FOREVERISM."[18]

The briefing explained the benefits of maintaining one's forever presence: that is, publicly sharing one's digital identity and keeping it updated. It suggested that forever presence is possible today thanks to "technology that allows [consumers and businesses] to find, follow, interact and collaborate forever with anyone & anything," like social media, which TrendWatching likened to "an eternally up-to-date encyclopedia of individuals." Social media profiles "will live on forever," along with "billions of other digital crumbs scattered across cyberspace," because "younger generations will never want to dispose of their groomed online presence to begin with." Those who use social media — "which in mature consumer societies will mean 99% of the population" — will have a "forever presence." This is a positive development, according to the briefing, because "What's forever present, is forever findable and trackable, too."[19]

Individuals online don't just stay forever present, they can converse with each other forever, too. This "conversation revolution" started by social media platforms has facilitated conversations among "friends, family, strangers, foes, and yes, brands, in every possible combination until the end of times." The briefing contended that consumers have always conversed with companies, but the "real-time, in-your-face, mass public conversation" occurring online has proven to be a better way for consumers to interact directly, and constantly, with brands (as well as celebrities). If someone wants to make a suggestion, file a complaint, or ask a question, they can tweet at the company or tag them in a post. And others can join the conversation, too, if they see the tagged post on their home page.[20]

Finally, the briefing called for an endless collaboration between consumers and companies, for thinking of the process as the product, and for prioritizing the unfinished over the final — in short, for adopting a "beta attitude." In a section titled "Forever Beta," it suggested that providing feedback to brands will publicly reveal their flaws but that brands should be open to "introducing and revealing themselves, flaws and all." If a user posts about a mistake a brand makes, the brand will have to acknowledge and rectify it. A "looping, continuous dialogue" will occur between consumers and brands, and to maintain a good relationship with consumers, brands will need to operate in a "humble, transparent, unpolished, almost human-like FOREVER BETA mode."[21]

This short memo from the ad world proved to be quite prescient. Intended to help marketers come up with new strategies, it described a discourse with enormous influence today. Individuals who are forever trackable, conversations that are never finished, products that are constantly being updated — these were capitalist ideals long before the TrendWatching briefing, and they continue to be perpetuated under capitalism. The briefing merely put a name to a set of statements, beliefs, attitudes, values, and processes already circulating. However, it failed to consider the potential pitfalls of these ideals. What are the consequences of remaining forever present, operating in a forever beta mode, and conversing forever? How do the tenets of forever-ism shape both the corporate sector and our lives? Does the forever work alongside or against the instant "now" culture of capitalism? And what happens when nothing ever ends?

It might seem vulgar to adopt a term created by marketers to describe some of the conditions of late capitalism. But marketing and advertising terms can describe negative conditions without necessarily meaning to. I'm reading the same words in the TrendWatching briefing as any marketer would, but where they might see possible strategies to promote brands, I — as a critic of consumer capitalism — see possibilities for exclusion, control, and oppression. This amounts to a difference in perception but also a disagreement over the purpose of marketing, which, for TrendWatching, is to serve businesses. But for me, the purpose of marketing is to maintain corporate dominance over our lives, to package brands with specific discourses that speak to the public but that serve ultimately to disenfranchise the working and middle classes and funnel wealth to the minority of individuals who own major corporations. In short, I find *foreverism* to be a useful term, just not in the same way TrendWatching does.

My argument in this book is that foreverism has replaced the older positivist discourses against nostalgia by proving to be a vital solution to a longstanding problem under capitalism: how to extinguish nostalgia while also profiting from it. But although foreverism appears less harsh than the punitive measures proposed by yesterday's positivists, its mission is still to suppress any emotional expression that might threaten the capitalist directives to work and produce, including the work needed to keep the past alive in the present. When nothing ever ends, the feelings associated with endings are muted — positive feelings such as the contentment and relief felt after finishing something, but sometimes also sadness, pain, grief, and of course nostalgia, especially when something ends that we didn't want to end. Foreverism promises to relieve those feelings while also making it quite difficult for us to rest knowing that the work is done, the case is closed, the story is over.

In what follows, I aim to explain why foreverism has become a dominant discourse in contemporary culture and politics, the effects foreverism has on our conception of nostalgia in particular, and the consequences of living in a time when nothing ever ends.

2

Everything Not Saved Will Be Lost

There is a difference between preservation and foreverizing, and a difference between foreverizing and restoration, that should be noted. All three are less punitive strategies to alleviate the nostalgic subject's bittersweet longing for the past, but they are no less tenacious in their mission to loosen nostalgia's grip — and they usually end up reinforcing the very longing they try to cure.

Preservation, Restoration, Foreverizing

Preservation starts with the impulse to save things. Decontextualize an object and place it behind glass, seal it in amber, lower the temperature to a degree freezing enough to halt all organic activity, enclose it in a vault, collect it with others and arrange them to be visible and admired, then charge admission. The process has its origins in the nineteenth century's "economy of desire": the spectacularization of objects, the commodification of the winsome, when the quaint and very small became fetishized.[1] The dizzying spiral of keepsakes, souvenirs, curio cabinets — these private objects turned living spaces into museums, where "domestic daydreaming and armchair nostalgia" could be indulged.[2]

The problem is that which is preserved must "die," so to speak, to be protected. It must be frozen in rigor mortis; it cannot exist in its context without risking patination. Neither can it truly live. "A culture that is merely preserved is no culture at all," Mark Fisher told us.[3] This presents a problem: one longs to be able to interact with the preserved thing, to live with it, but it must be protected from time, must exist so close but so far away. Restoration, on the other hand, involves cleaning up something old to make it look new, or better than new. But the restoration can only last so long before it will need restoring once again.

Let me provide an example from popular music to illustrate the differences between preservation, restoration, and foreverizing: the long-running American rock band Lynyrd Skynyrd. Formed in the 1960s, Lynyrd Skynyrd has enjoyed success thanks in part to its willingness to foreverize itself against aging and death, as well as the fan labor to keep the spirit of the band alive through time. To preserve Lynyrd Skynyrd's music is to keep the band's physical media safe from aging, perhaps by framing one of their vinyl records and hanging it on a wall. Prized Lynyrd Skynyrd memorabilia can also be preserved by placing it behind glass or in a museum. Some of the band's original tapes are stored in an air-conditioned room in a house belonging to Tom Markham, regarded as the first to record the band in the late 1960s.[4] These are all preservation tactics; the point is to freeze pieces of the band in time. To restore Lynyrd Skynyrd's music is to remix and remaster it to meet modern-day audio standards. As a result, the music sounds cleaner and clearer, maybe even louder and better, than it originally did. It's a more interactive approach than preservation and gives the feeling that one is encountering them for the first time again. But to foreverize

Lynyrd Skynyrd is to add new members to the band when older members leave or pass away, something they've been doing in earnest since their reformation in the late 1980s following the deadly 1977 plane crash that killed three of their members. Lynyrd Skynyrd could also foreverize themselves by allowing contemporary producers to remix their hits for marketing purposes. The 2022 TOTEM remix of "Free Bird" is a perfect example of foreverizing. TOTEM describes itself as a "boutique music library" that produces cinematic music for theatrical marketing.[5] Its remix of "Free Bird" is designed to penetrate new marketing channels and generate new sources of income, ultimately aiding in the franchising of the band. The remix sounds like Hans Zimmer covering Skynyrd: pounding drums, huge strings, and a plummeting moment of silence before the guitar-led outro kicks in. Across its 3:00 runtime, you can almost see the trailer to a blockbuster action film flash before your eyes.

One is reminded of the Ship of Theseus story when encountering a foreverized product. If all the original parts of a ship are replaced with new ones, is it still the same ship? Is Lynyrd Skynyrd still Lynyrd Skynyrd with the members of their classic lineup replaced? By continually adding new members, the band never has to stop touring and recording music unless they want to. They could just as easily replenish themselves over and over again with new talent, essentially ensuring their continued longevity in the future. The tactic resembles other forms of foreverizing in popular music: holograms of famous deceased artists that perform their hits live; writing camps sponsored by music investment firms, where songwriters are invited to compose prospective hits by interpolating older songs, the rights of which are owned by the firms; and artists continuing to tour after their supposed "farewell" tours.

Foreverism maintains that the old can't be merely preserved or re-released; it must be revived, given new stories, de-aged to provide the illusion of vitality, updated, rebooted. The impulse to foreverize content might be driven by nostalgia initially, but in practice, by keeping things forever present, it can eliminate the conditions of yearning. After all, can we really pin the blame for so many ludicrous reboots on the public's nostalgia for them?

It might seem like a nostalgic demand for older content is the reason for all the rebooting, like the numerous revivals of *The Munsters*, an American sitcom about a family of monsters that ran from 1964 to 1966. Much to my surprise, the 2022 Rob Zombie–directed reboot of *The Munsters* was not the first time the series was rebooted. Several film adaptations were released through the second half of the twentieth century: *Munster, Go Home!* in 1966, *The Mini-Munsters* in 1973, *The Munsters' Revenge* in 1981, *Here Come the Munsters* in 1995, and *The Munsters' Scary Little Christmas* in 1996. *The Munsters Today* premiered in 1988 and ran for three seasons until 1991. And in 2012, a reboot series called *Mockingbird Lane* was scrapped after the pilot aired. In short, like so many other franchises, rebooting *The Munsters* isn't a twenty-first century development.

But was nostalgia for *The Munsters* the reason for its many reboots? Perhaps, but who can say with certainty? When reboots are announced, there is the usual accusation of nostalgia. But they aren't necessarily a reaction to our nostalgia for them; instead, they aim to prevent stories from disappearing into the past by providing fans access to their intellectual properties.

Although *The Munsters* franchise has tried to keep its characters forever present since 1964, no company has succeeded at foreverizing its own content more than Disney, which owns both the Marvel Cinematic Universe (MCU) and *Star Wars*. For many decades, Disney's strategy was to preserve, and sometimes restore, its classics, but now its mission is foreverizing. The shift can be seen in Disney's decision to retire the Disney Vault, a strategy whereby Disney released some of its titles on home video for a limited time before placing them back into the vault. Consumers flocked to buy restored classics when Disney took them out of the vault, never knowing with certainty if or when they'd be made available again. Otherwise, consumers would have to search the secondhand market for their favorite vaulted film. With the 2019 launch of Disney+, the company's streaming platform, the Disney Vault was officially retired. All of its classic titles, from *Bambi* to *Beauty and the Beast*, would be available to stream on the platform.

The Disney Vault framed some of Disney's most famous works as scarce objects. When they were placed in the vault, they were inaccessible to the public. This very likely inspired nostalgia in viewers wishing to own a classic title on physical media. In other words, vaultification made possible the conditions for nostalgia, while Disney+ allows those films to be accessed at any time, effectively preventing viewers from longing for them. By replacing scarcity with accessibility, Disney is suggesting that it isn't a matter of *if* you're going to watch an animated classic, but *when*.

Accessibility is only one of Disney's foreverizing strategies. The company also produces new content based on their works, not only making them more available than they were during vaultification, but also rebooting them with new stories, characters, and settings. Take *Star Wars* as an example. Every new *Star Wars* reboot triggers an avalanche of thinkpieces reflecting on, praising, or criticizing the nostalgia of the franchise. But like *The Munsters* reboots, are the *Star Wars* installments made to profit off viewers' nostalgia or to prevent fans from ever missing *Star Wars* again?

If you were alive between the original trilogy and the prequel trilogy, then you might have longed for newer *Star Wars* movies. So what happened? *Star Wars* fans got three new movies, several anthology films, and even more live-action series to satisfy a possible nostalgic craving, and there are so many more in development. Think about it: how can anyone be nostalgic for *Star Wars* when there's a new film or series released every year? If nostalgia is the emotion experienced when the past briefly reappears in the present, then it cannot accurately describe the feeling associated with consuming *Star Wars* when it appears on screens, merchandising, and advertising of all kinds all the time.

This strategy of foreverizing *Star Wars* does not prevent Disney from claiming that *Star Wars* is worth longing for; it merely provides the justification for an endless stream of Lucasfilm content, so that the series never disappears into the past. The irony, of course, is that by framing *Star Wars* as something to be nostalgic for, Disney is implicitly arguing that nothing new can top *Star Wars*. It's a cycle: new *Star Wars* films prevent the franchise from disappearing into the past, while also suggesting that new movies can never match *Star Wars*.

In an interview with *Vanity Fair*, aptly titled "*Star Wars* Forever," Lucasfilm president and producer Kathleen Kennedy called the studio's approach to producing *Star Wars* movies "persistent storytelling," the production of narratives that don't conform to traditional trilogy arcs but, instead, continue indefinitely.[6] Old characters appear in new stories; new characters take up the mantle; friends square off against foes. These are stories that endure (simply because they're enormously successful), so there is an assumption made by Lucasfilm that audiences will invest in them and want more. Persistent storytelling pressures the public into accepting a new *Star Wars* movie as the next important thing, an event that can't be missed, but that often recedes quickly from public memory shortly after the ads stop.

When persistent storytelling becomes standard practice, something crucial disappears: endings. With no end to the *Star Wars* universe in sight, it can be quite difficult to experience nostalgia for *Star Wars* — unless you long for the rush of watching the original for the first time again. Seeking that rush might be enough of a reason to watch new *Star Wars* installments, but Lucasfilm knows you can't go back. Instead, it provides fans with new movies and series in an attempt to satisfy any nostalgic craving. But like most attempts to diminish nostalgia, the result might be a more acute case of it.

In her essay "Nostalgia for Nostalgia," Alexandra Fiorentino-Swinton laments the death of finality in narrative cinema, noting the utter strangeness of films like *Stand by Me* or *The Breakfast Club* — films that come to an end without sequels, prequels, or reboots. "The first time I watched *The Breakfast Club*," she writes, "I immediately started thinking of what might have happened next, wanting to believe in some fan-fiction-worthy scenario in which they met up at school on Monday morning and proceeded to become a 'found family' kind of friend group." She notes that narrative practices have changed in an era of continuity, when a premium is placed on franchising and expansion:

> In popular entertainments marketed to me, stories are supposed to go on forever — bolstered by endless spin-offs and fan extensions. Some of my favorite franchises like the *Avengers* and *Star Wars* have spent recent years trading on their own history, with callback upon callback creating a feedback loop out of their legacies.[7]

This obsession with narrative continuity mirrors the foreverizing of our relationships in the

"The difference between movies and television is that movies have an ending," film critic A. S. Hamrah noted in a 2022 interview. Otherwise, he argues, movies without endings are just soap operas. "There's something childish and juvenile about things that don't end," he said. "It just opens itself up to be repetitive, those are the characteristics of television. Right away, there's a difference between the two forms that people don't really want to acknowledge."[9] Persistent storytelling provides audiences with the childish experience of limitlessness, and if there is nostalgia being felt, it is likely for that experience. Endings are regarded as uncomfortable shocks, challenges to the technocratic imperative to accept the latest update, the newest development. Incremental changes, but nothing that would rock the entire cinematic franchise, are tolerated. Continuity is celebrated.

A paradoxical consequence of this quest for perfect continuity is that many of the storylines of cinematic universes have become flagrantly complex. Only the most learned fans can hope to keep track of every development, which is arguably part of the appeal. The reboots with the most hidden references, or "Easter eggs," are perfect for the diehard fans to dissect. The latest installment in a popular universe functions as a massive game of spot-the-references, where fans can cosplay as conspiracists, connect the dots, list the hidden clues, and draw bold lines between them to graph a shape of its history, a foreverist gesture that can only be made in a milieu where the artifacts of older cultures haunt the present. Watching new installments, with all their references to the older ones, is like weaving the present into history, not only to give one a sense of progress in a time running out of it, but also to foreverize the past: to keep it alive and growing forever.

The "forever presence" of cinematic universes also keeps the people involved — the cast and crew, the marketing and public relations departments — forever present as well, locked into their own roles to ensure the universe keeps expanding. One consequence of this lock-in is that actors play the same roles for years in these universes, sometimes at the expense of more creatively fulfilling endeavors. But another consequence is that filmmaking has become increasingly digitized, so that a greater amount of control can be exercised over the creative process. In practice digitization allows for retroactive continuity, or retconning, to maintain continuity through recontextualization, for hiding Easter eggs in post-production, and for last-minute rewriting to interlace references and keep things straight. Without digitization, a franchise couldn't be easily foreverized. And as a result of these practices, actors can sometimes find themselves in surreal situations on set.

Instead of delivering his lines from a mountaintop, as he mostly did shooting Peter Jackson's *Lord of the Rings* trilogy, Ian McKellen found himself on a digital backlot, surrounded by green screen, while filming *The Hobbit*. The veteran actor who played Gandalf grew frustrated with the unreal setting:

> In order to shoot the dwarves and a large Gandalf, we couldn't be in the same set. All I had for company was thirteen photographs of the dwarves on top of stands with little lights — whoever's talking flashes up. Pretending you're with thirteen other people when you're on your own, it stretches your technical ability to the absolute limits . . . And I cried, actually. I cried. Then I said out loud, "This is not why I became an actor."[10]

McKellen, a seven-time winner of the Laurence Olivier Award, has played Richard III, Iago,

Macbeth, and Romeo on film and the world's most prestigious stages. But on the set of *The Hobbit* he was miserable. "It may be my impression but I don't remember a green screen on *The Lord of the Rings*," he remarked. "If Gandalf was on top of a mountain, I'd be there on the mountain."[11]

Jackson incorporated green screen during the filming of the original trilogy, but for *The Hobbit* installments, he pushed the technique to its limit, leading many fans and critics to prefer the former trilogy over the latter. (There was also the criticism that Jackson had stretched the single volume of *The Hobbit* over three movies and nearly eight hours of run time.) Agreeing to return as Gandalf, McKellen performed on a blank, spiritless set so that a digitally rendered world could be applied in post-production using the latest visual effects technology. More than an exercise in displaying new effects, however, the films' reliance on green screens, as well as its protracted run time, allowed for a degree of control absent from the original trilogy.

McKellen hasn't been the only veteran actor to struggle on the set of a major movie franchise. In a radio interview, Jake Gyllenhaal admitted that he had trouble remembering his lines as Mysterio while filming 2019's *Spider-Man: Far From Home*. When the host suggested that Gyllenhaal wasn't challenged by the filming, with its green screens and simplistically macho performances, Gyllenhaal quickly corrected him:

> It's hard, man. That acting is hard. All of it. That world is enormous . . . For me, normally, I come in way early on, and I get to play and I get to figure it out. It was like, you gotta deliver in that space. And it was a whole different craft.

The enormous world he was referring to is the Marvel Cinematic Universe (MCU), Marvel Studios' collection of superhero films and series. Filming the Spider-Man installment, he said, was like joining a "train that was already moving." He explained that the filmmakers would sometimes change an entire day's schedule to accommodate a new idea if someone on set had one. This led to difficulties remembering his lines. He eventually sought support from actor Tom Holland, who, while playing the part of Spider-Man, helped to ease Gyllenhaal's anxieties.[12]

Ian McKellen and Jake Gyllenhaal found themselves laboring in a new kind of cinematic system, one that remains strictly controlled and that cannot, without good incentive, come to an end. It must remain forever present, and to do so requires enormous technical control to maintain continuity, to keep the storytelling persistent.

To provide the strictest of controls, these films rely on green screen and towering video walls like Industrial Light & Magic's StageCraft to build and edit flexible, otherworldly environments. Actors perform on lime green stages, or on Volumes: combination LED walls and soundstages. The worlds in these films are designed in post-production or displayed onscreen around the actors. ILM's "Brain Bar," a crew of visual effects designers on set, can tweak the Volume's display in real time, editing live animations and color-correcting the background projected onscreen to match the actual design elements on set. The Volume eliminates the impersonal environment of the green screen while providing an adaptable soundstage for showrunners to maintain continuity.

Armed with this level of control, filmmakers can produce franchise films more efficiently, without actors or effects crew grumbling about the coldness of a green screen. But there is a tradeoff: actors are awarded a more tangible set but are more firmly locked in the franchise. They will earn enormous wealth at the cost of other creative desires, a creative tension as old as the movie business. But once they agree to take a role in a cinematic universe, they will discover that they aren't acting in a movie but in something else.

Like the *Lord of the Rings* franchise, the MCU doesn't produce films in the traditional sense; it produces content. Content has no ending. It is consumable but inexhaustible. The production of Marvel films is like the infinite scroll: one watches them in a steady stream, which is always replenishing itself without end. The irony is that content is easily consumed but quickly forgotten. The more that content is created to prevent a cinematic universe from undergoing its own big crunch, the less likely we are to remember it once it's replaced by the next installment, the next story in the universe. Attempting to relieve nostalgia, cinematic universes end up creating a kind of selective amnesia: throwaway reboots are either forgotten or written out of the canon, but originals are usually remembered fondly. Nostalgia for *The Breakfast Club*, and all those high-school feelings associated with it, can't be alleviated by a two-season streaming reboot. Perhaps we know this, deep down. Maybe that's why there hasn't been a reboot of it yet.

After Peter Jackson directed *The Hobbit* trilogy, he made the World War I documentary *They Shall Not Grow Old*. The film was lauded for its restoration techniques. Writing for *The Guardian*, Peter Bradshaw called the documentary "eerie" and "hyperreal" and the soldiers brought to colorized life "like ghosts or figures summoned up in a séance."[13] The prevailing opinion among many critics was that Jackson had brought us closer to the action and thus closed the gap between past and present, to give audiences the feeling of actually being there, in colored and pristine detail.

Film historian Luke McKernan thought differently:

> Colourisation does not bring us closer to the past; it increases the gap between now and then. It does not enable immediacy; it creates difference. It makes the past record all the more distant for rejecting what is honest about it. If we want to encourage a new generation to understand what the war meant — and of course this is a good

thing — we should be inviting them to look at the films as they were made and through that effort to appreciate them for what they are, and what they meant in their time . . . Film that looks like it was shot last week belongs only to last week.[14]

I kept thinking of that quote while watching Jackson's 2021 docuseries, *The Beatles: Get Back*, which captures in stunning detail the Fab Four in the studio working on *Let It Be*. The docuseries was also praised for its restoration techniques, which used artificial intelligence to bring the band to life in a way that is uncannily clear, as if you're in the room with them. The restoration is so polished that when my wife and I first saw the trailer for it, she remarked, "Are they actors or is that really them?"

The Beatles: Get Back isn't a documentary. It does not present a record of the past; it foreverizes the past through intensive restoration techniques, thus making the past feel more present. It is like watching artificial intelligence apply movement to a photo of a deceased loved one: the face moves, but the result is uncanny. It demixes the audio of these famed studio sessions so that the individual voices and instruments of the Beatles can be heard clearly, producing never-before-heard conversations for fans and ensuring fans' conversations, comments, and even criticisms about the Beatles will continue. It frames the Beatles as something to be improved for a more enjoyable experience in the present day, positing that there is something lacking, deficient even, in the band worth updating. This approach is the beta attitude applied to the most famous rock band in history, and it doesn't bring us closer to the past, it distances us from it.

They Shall Not Grow Old and *The Beatles: Get Back* are Jackson's attempts to foreverize two pieces of history, World War I and the Beatles; to not only restore them through colorization and remastering but also de-age them with artificial intelligence. It's a foreverizing process that allows producers to squeeze the last dollars out of past creations and achieve a kind of immortality by reanimating old intellectual properties.

Any medium is historically contextualized. Producers like Jackson know this. That's why he worked for years on restoring the Beatles footage. But it seems that some regard a medium as merely a conduit through which the past can be transmitted, and that if we make it more transparent, if we simply remove its dirt and dust, then the real thing will shine through. But Jackson didn't wipe the dirt off the past to reveal any truth. He merely created simulations that look like the real past. As Luke McKernan argued, he cleaned up what was honest about the footage of the past and instead created a record of the present.

At the end of Kathleen Kennedy's *Vanity Fair* interview, she talks about the Producers Guild of America (PGA) Milestone Award she and George Lucas won in 2022. To honor the two, the PGA made a highlight video spanning their career together:

> The team cut this reel together, and I just looked at it a couple of days ago. First of all, I don't know where they found some of the footage. It goes *way* back. But what I was so taken with is how much *fun* we were having. It amounted to this moment of realization: I do think a little bit of fun has gone out of making these gigantic movies. The business, the stakes, everything that's been infused in the last 10 years or so. There's a kind of spontaneity and good time that we have to be careful to preserve. I keep holding on to: It better be fun.[15]

New stories are often very exciting. When they become franchises and the point is to maintain their continuity, the fun, as Kennedy suggests, can disappear. The methods to create them change, too. Accidents are allowed less and less; to control for them, actors may find themselves alone speaking to cardboard cutouts on lime-green sets, or surrounded by vast screens that purport to immerse them in alien environments.

Rebooting intellectual properties is merely a first step. Then they must be maintained. They must be recirculated, with new stories folded in. One must be persistent so that the intellectual property doesn't slip away into the past, to join the other memories we've forgotten but that, upon witnessing them flash by in a highlight reel, remind us how much happier we really were back then. Persistent storytelling prevents nostalgia from setting in, just like the financialization of older pop music, where aging pop stars sell their back catalogues to investment funds, who flood their music across the culture and rake in streaming royalties. Fleetwood Mac's ubiquity across commercials, social media, playing in brick-and-mortar stores, and so on doesn't merely indicate a general nostalgia for Fleetwood Mac. It is a result of their catalogue sale to music investment firms Hipgnosis, Primary Wave, and BMG, whose job it is to carpet-bomb the cultural landscape with Fleetwood Mac or any other artist who signs a deal with them.[16] Whatever method is used to keep the IP from disappearing, and then reappearing as a ghostly reminder of the loss, will work. Those of us unaccustomed to such revitalization might ponder its authenticity: are they really the Beatles? Is this really *Star Wars*? Are we really nostalgic, or have we forgotten the sensation?

Forever Is a Place on Earth

Some things are considered failures if they don't last forever, or if they're expected not to last. Relationships fall apart, businesses go under, your favorite series airs its final episode or gets cancelled. There are lucrative industries today offering services to help individuals stay in touch with friends, maintain their businesses, keep their relationships going, prolong their lives. Fantastical theories are put forth to extend human life, from uploading our minds to computers to freezing our bodies at cryogenic temperatures.

Singularitists believe that humans could one day meld with machines, while virtual reality promoters promise a digital heaven where uploaded consciousness could frolic forever. When movies and series end, there is always the possibility of a sequel or a reboot. In an economic system where growth is the ultimate goal, things that do not, or cannot, grow forever are often criticized. But the truth is, not everything can last forever.

While these industries attempt to make things everlasting, capitalism at large thrives on disposability, ephemerality, planned obsolescence, and short-lived desires. Digital technologies programmed to degrade, fast fashion, and single-use plastic are just three examples of things that allegedly do not last forever. Yet, in reality, they do — they just last forever somewhere else. Take, for example, an action performed by many people daily: throwing away a plastic water bottle. Where does it go once we've thrown it "away"? It seems to disappear, no longer here now and forever out of sight. But as writer and activist George Monbiot reminds us, "There is no 'away,' it's still on this planet."[17] The plastic bottle doesn't really go away, it just moves from one place to another. It travels from our sight to somewhere out of sight, from the now to a forever uncomfortable to many who ponder the environment and sustainability.

A lot of what is thrown away ends up in landfills and our oceans. Plastic six-pack yokes break down into microplastics that humans and other animals might ingest. Landfilled e-waste, like old smartphones and computers, leaches heavy metals and "forever chemicals," or per- and polyfluoroalkyl substances, into the soil. A 2020 paper found that cell phones, ammunition, firefighting foam, and guitar strings are just a few sources of forever chemicals, some of which are extremely persistent and may take centuries to break down.[18]

The "Foreverism" TrendWatching publication suggested that moving consumer society away from the "now" might be more environmentally friendly. Instead of replacing something when it goes bad, consumers could purchase a specific part. Instead of buying a new and improved smartphone, consumers could buy a particular module to update it. The briefing also advocated for long-lasting hardware to run on "non-polluting" software that is continually updated. But there is no mention of how this would be more environmentally sound. The foreverism of long-lasting products and the nowism of single-use plastic aren't mutually exclusive; they both strain the planet. This is troubling to those who associate the now with disposability and the forever with growth.

And both foreverism and nowism have the effect of forestalling nostalgia. If foreverism works to keep things from disappearing into the past (and thus prevents the first step towards feeling nostalgic), nowism tries to preclude us from feeling nostalgic for an older thing by replacing it with something new. Attachments to older technologies or fashions might be severed with the arrival of an updated device or a new clothing trend. The desire to appear in step with trends might drive us to quickly dismiss, or throw away, old items. But that doesn't mean our nostalgia for them goes away.

That which is promised to last forever might not, and that which is here today and gone tomorrow might last forever, or at least a disturbingly long time. Of all the things that remain forever present, perhaps the most disturbing is nuclear waste. Estimates range widely on how long it should be stored. Ten thousand years? A million years? The shocking truth is that no one, not even the experts, really knows the answer. Spent fuel is often buried deep in the earth, a short-term solution that doesn't bode well for the future. Some scientists hope that advances in containment technology will present functional long-term storage solutions in the future, as if the technology will one day fall into their lap. It's a risky gamble, considering that future inhabitants of our planet may not understand the language in which nuclear warning labels are written. Ludicrous schemes of "nuclear semiotics" are proposed, like the "ray cat solution": breeding cats that will glow green when exposed to radiation, indicating the location of unknown pockets of nuclear waste — a feline warning sign that future humans are somehow expected to recognize. How do you signal to a person one hundred thousand years from now that a giant, subterranean container holds toxic waste? A better question might be, will there be any humans around to notice? Only in a foreverist society would people assume that humans will last forever.

Nuclear waste threatens foreverist thinking because it challenges the belief that forever equates with progress, so it's often hidden from view, buried deep underground — out of sight, out of mind. Like all everlasting things that complicate our fragile progress narratives, nuclear waste depends on relative invisibility. To glimpse it is to call foreverism into question. Only that which lasts happily forever is paraded before the public by elites eager to clap for progress. But even the apparently less destructive promises of forever aren't completely immaterial. Foreverism is transcendent merely in theory. It always relies on earthbound processes and hard labor.

Let's consider another example that reveals foreverism's shaky promises and antinostalgic tendencies: data centers. Servers across all the world's data centers, referred to as "the cloud," hold countless images, videos, content, and all kinds of information, some of which are framed as "memories." Digital transfer companies such as Forever Studios and iMemories offer services to save one's analog memories forever in the cloud. I briefly mentioned earlier about how iMemories promises to "foreverize your memories" by digitizing home movies recorded on VHS and storing them in the cloud to be accessed on any device.[19] Customers of digital transfer companies rely on

about not accumulating everything."[22] Yet the cloud provides the illusion that perhaps everything *can* be saved, when maybe it *can't* — a lesson learned in 2017 by the Library of Congress when it announced it was ending its project to archive every tweet simply because there were too many tweets.[23]

Data storage encourages indiscriminate foreverizing: you never know what you might miss in the future, so the best practice is to save it all. The point isn't necessarily to preserve information but to keep information in an accessible location for us to interact with forever. This model of total foreverizing is, as Hogan notes, "currently set to fail because it denies its own limitations."[24] A planetary politics for everyone will require some kind of appraisal of information, some deliberation over what should be saved and what should be forgotten.

No one knows how many data centers exist around the world, but they hide in plain sight. Like nuclear storage facilities, they aren't entirely invisible. They, instead, are rhetorically hidden, elided into "the cloud" and other phrases meant to obscure their material impact and vulnerability. They save great quantities of information, but just because we might have access to information now doesn't mean that information will always be readily accessible. Data centers are prone to breaches, leaks, and deletions. We are told that data is stored forever in the cloud, but it can be wiped away accidentally, as was the case when over 50 million songs uploaded to MySpace disappeared during a server migration project in 2019.[25] And if Amazon Web Services (AWS) wants to kick a company, or a government, off its servers, it can. Or, if a server suffers an outage, like a northern Virginia network did in late 2020, security cameras, credit card companies, and energy businesses can all go dark.[26] The Central Intelligence Agency relies on AWS to support workloads across all levels of classification, including Top Secret information. What happens if these servers are compromised?

Framing images and videos as "memories" isn't a new phenomenon. Home movies on VHS are considered memories to many families who still own and have access to their tapes. What is relatively new is the rate at which "memories" are being saved in the cloud. Digital "memories" accumulate online, on our devices, in the cloud: all flattened into moments you must remember, moments that shouldn't be missed, moments that can be accessed at any time. And yet, the sheer quantity of these "memories" is often so overwhelming that it can cause choice paralysis, preventing us from accessing and remembering them. Like all forms of foreverizing, the digitization of "memories" attempts to eliminate nostalgia by keeping the past accessible but ends up eliciting it instead.

As the TrendWatching briefing noted, foreverism might appear more environmentally sustainable. Its framing as "non-polluting" depends upon the assumption that something can't last forever on a planet too hot to accommodate life. But foreverism doesn't necessarily present a "clean" alternative to the nowism of capitalism. In fact, it threatens the planet as much as nowism does.

To illustrate this point, let's consider electric vehicles. Although they might appear "clean," electric vehicles don't solve the climate crisis any more than data centers do because both rely on energy grids powered by fossil fuels. As writer Paris Marx notes in *Road to Nowhere*, electric vehicles "only appear clean and green because environmental messaging narrowly focuses on tailpipe emissions, ignoring the harm that pervades the supply chain and the unsustainable nature of auto-oriented development."[27] Charging stations in the US are primarily powered by fossil fuels, and the cobalt used in the batteries of electric vehicles is often mined by children in heavily polluted conflict zones such as the Democratic Republic of Congo.[28] Even though electric vehicles don't produce tailpipe emissions, their production does harm to individuals and the environments in which they live.

And yet, electric vehicles are often argued as the future of automobility as the climate crisis worsens. The Zero Emission Vehicle mandate in the UK has aimed to phase out gas-powered vehicles and replace them with zero-emissions vehicles by 2035, the same deadline by which the US government hopes most vehicles operated by its federal agencies will be electric. But although some electric vehicles are designed to look futuristic to match the future-facing rhetoric of their proponents, others are modeled after classic gas-powered automobiles. Jaguar's E-type Zero is modeled after its classic E-type, which was produced in the 1960s and 1970s and was recently showcased in AMC's hit series *Mad Men*. The

E-type Zero was Jaguar's attempt to "future-proof classic-car ownership" — in other words, to provide the exhilarating feeling of owning a vintage car while also adhering to proposed zero-emissions mandates.[29] There's also Ford's F-100 Eluminator, an electric vehicle modeled after its 1978 F-100 pickup truck. It looks somewhat classic, but it sports EV technology.

These retro EVs don't merely restore classic designs; restoration involves scrubbing away the patina of the past to bring it back like brand new, maybe even better than it was when it was first introduced. To foreverize a 1978 F-100 is to produce a new truck that looks like the old one but with new mechanics to hopefully ensure its survival in a future free from fossil fuels. A restored F-100 might still break down due to wear and tear; it might have been restored, but it's still old. A foreverized vehicle, however, is newly produced. It promises years of driving time, not just today but in the future if companies ban gas-powered vehicle purchases. It's a reboot, a promising new development set in the same old world of traffic jams and conflict minerals. But like so many reboots, it's just not the same as the original, and it doesn't quiet all those problematic feelings: the nostalgia for the original, the anxiety for the future.

Foreverism isn't immaterial. Although the concept of forever carries transcendent implications, while the now appears so much more tangible, material, and bodily, these are always shifting associations. The imperative to "live in the present" is perhaps as transcendent as the promise that one's love will last forever. They are not so different. Both the now and the forever have planetary consequences that affect us *now*. But when the past is collapsed into the present, and everything is future-proofed, you might feel powerless to take action.

3

Trapped In The Present

Living according to foreverist ideals — to be forever present, upgrading, and conversing — can be an exhausting existence. You experience the feeling of stasis, of being stuck, as if nothing ever gets done (nothing's ever *done*), as well as the jetlag of constant motion. You must always remain vigilant so you don't ever "miss" anything, always improving, perfecting, grinding, hustling, and moving up, so you're never done with work. As TrendWatching noted, the "process is the product." Betterment, however, does not mean change in a foreverist society. You must grow but also be continuous with yourself, to keep your "forever presence," because foreverist societies would like to maintain continuity to keep things trackable. Individuals are incentivized to brand themselves on social media, exchanging a performance of inflexibility for likes, followers, partnerships, endorsements. Staying true to one's brand, and unable to exercise much autonomy, a person trapped in a foreverist society can feel as though they are a character in a cinematic universe, or an icon in a game played by someone else, or like they're laboring in a virtual simulation. Players search for exits out of the "game" but are confronted by borders, bureaucracies, checkpoints.

Maintenance of the status quo is privileged over progress in a foreverist society. Legislation to improve the lives of the working class isn't passed; debt keeps people stuck in place, unable to move forward; people feel out of control in their own lives. Meanwhile, capitalism maintains growth of profit for the elites while telling the rest of us that insignificant, incremental updating is the best that can be done. Action is limited, pre-determined, forecasted. It seems there is nothing you can do.

Not If, But When

This feeling of inevitable entrapment is often expressed in a phrase that commonly repeats in public discourse today: "It's not a matter of if, but when." I started noticing the phrase some-time during the COVID-19 lockdowns of 2020. I remember the Centers for Disease Control warning Americans that it wasn't a matter of *if* COVID-19 would disrupt our lives, but *when* it would. The phrase, with its threat-level aura, was then applied to every conceivable danger: cyber-attacks, economic crashes, data breaches, the next pandemic. I heard my father say it during a con-versation about one of the COVID variants in 2021. Friends have said it, usually frustrated by some inevitable change coming to their careers: "My hands are tied at work. It's not a matter of if my job will be restructured, but when . . . "

According to the statement, these crises were destined to happen. The speakers of the phrase, assuming the role of negative prophets, were tell-ing us that bad things were going to occur whether we liked it or not. At best we could hunker down and accept our fate. When a Medscape article declared that it wasn't a matter of if a radiation oncology department would be the next victim of a cyberattack, but when, the author was demonstrating that these attacks are "increasing in frequency and magnitude" — which is to say, they're already here, they're getting worse, and we might be too vulnerable to stop them.[1] Prevention is futile. Only resilience can save us now.

To utter "not if, but when" is to announce a determined future into existence and to silence any objections. At best, it can give attention to the concerning issues bearing down on us, but rarely are any alternatives offered to thwart, or at least mitigate, the harm of *when*. Rather, it promises relative stasis: we must maintain through the harsh season, the endless winter. To the degree change is possible, it is negative: things will change, but the change will be for the worse. Meanwhile, corporate and military powers will make necessary changes to maintain the operability of markets, while the most vulnerable are expected to adopt a tough disposition, to make the necessary cuts to survive, and to do so without question and certainly without longing for the past.

The phrase reflects a weird viewpoint in the digital age: it is as if reality itself can be viewed like an ongoing series or cinematic franchise with each development framed as an inevitable plot. Characters die off, older narratives are rebooted, but the overarching structure of the series remains the same. The status quo remains forever present, while people are expected to survive — or even somehow to derive growth from — extreme, life-threatening conditions. Our perception is that someone else is controlling our lives, and why would it be any different? "Not if, but when" essentially locks us into assigned positions for the foreseeable future. This agency lock-in, combined with expectations that we quantify performance at work and home, navigate convoluted bureaucracies, and compete to earn salary raises, can make a person feel as if they're trapped in a game, controlled by a remote sadistic gamer.

Those of us feeling trapped are not automatons; rather, we are like characters in a story who have become aware of our entrapment. Some might enjoy living in a predetermined universe, one that's pre-written for them. Unless, of course, the universe is hostile; then they might endeavor to scale one level up from the simulation and into the real world. They would experience profound horror knowing they were locked in the wrong universe, the backwards world, the meaner reality.

John Scalzi's novel *Redshirts* provides a picture of what might happen if characters come to this shocking revelation. In the book, a group of inter-galactic ensigns aboard the spacecraft *Intrepid* start to suspect that they are actually characters in a television series. Andrew Dahl, the novel's protagonist, notices that the lower-ranked crew members die more often than the senior officers, who either escape dangerous situations unharmed or endure an exaggerated amount of trauma without dying. Crew members avoid the officers as much as they can, for if they accompany them on an away mission to the surface of a planet, they're likely to die in bizarre ways: "Death by falling rock. Death by toxic atmosphere. Death by pulse gun vaporization," to name a few.[2] Dahl is shocked to learn the veteran crew even has a name for this phenomenon: the Sacrificial Effect.

He observes other strange behaviors aboard the *Intrepid*. When he's tasked to produce a "counter-bacterial" to cure a plague ravaging an alien planet, he's given a box resembling a micro-wave oven in which he places a vial, closes the lid, and waits a few hours until it dings. He's then

instructed to run to the bridge, present the gib-
berish data scrolling on his tablet to the science
officer in person, and leave the bridge as soon
as possible. He also notices that fellow members will occasionally act more dramatically than
usual, only to snap back to normal, and he's told
to avoid "the Narrative" by a recluse on the ship.

Along with a group of fellow ensigns, Dahl
learns the truth of what's going on: their lives are
being influenced by the writers of *The Chronicles of
the Intrepid*, a series that premiered on basic cable
in 2007 and ran for several seasons. Everything
that happens in the show in some way happens
aboard the *Intrepid*. When a writer kills off a
character in the show, their double dies in real
life in the future. Dahl and the others are worried
that they too will be killed in horrible ways unless
they travel back in time and stop production on
the show.

The first half of the novel, before the twist is
revealed, explores the frustrations of military
bureaucracy, the lack of concern senior officers
have for their crew, and the sycophantic behaviors ensigns must display to the officers. When
ensigns are killed off, they're quickly replaced by
new ones. There is a steady pipeline of talent

funneling into the *Intrepid*, perpetual fodder for the death machine. Dahl is flabbergasted at how inefficiently and rigidly the *Intrepid* is run and questions why lower-ranking officers would even need to accompany senior officers on dangerous away missions. He also asks the other longstanding crew members if they've ever reported the unusually high casualty rate to the Military Bureau of Investigation, or to journalists, but nothing has come of it because there is no evidence that the leaders of the *Intrepid* are incompetent. It is just how things are: to be an ensign aboard the *Intrepid* is to inevitably die an untimely death, and there is nothing any of them can do about it. Their fates are sealed — or, as Dahl notes, "It's not a matter of *if* I get killed, it's when."[3]

Particularly disconcerting to Dahl is the sheer trauma that an officer, Lieutenant Kerensky, has endured every two months for three years without dying. "He should be in a fetal position by now," he tells a fellow ensign. "As it is, it's like he has just enough time to recover before he gets the shit kicked out of him again. He's unreal."[4] Kerensky is the model of resilience in the novel: able to suffer extreme injury but unable to die, the perfect worker in an uncaring system, a character with no time to experience painful emotions. He will endure whatever trauma is necessary to advance the plot.

The characters in *Redshirts* discover that all the systems of power have coordinated against them to keep the story in which they're trapped forever present. Some individuals are expendable and die quickly; others are expected to stay alive without tears or nostalgia for the ones they've lost. Facing such strange circumstances, they do about the only thing they can do: converse with each other constantly.

Scalzi writes almost the entire novel in dialogue. Characters are always saying something, always quipping and commenting, usually about the absurd things happening to them. The language Scalzi writes for his characters is similar to Whedonspeak, a style of dialogue popularized by writer Joss Whedon, whose credits include *Buffy the Vampire Slayer* and *The Cabin in the Woods*. Whedon is notorious for writing his characters as if they are vaguely aware they are acting in a fiction, or, at least, as if they are familiar with the dramatic tropes of television and feel the need to constantly comment on them. Characters in

Whedon's stories rarely stay silent but, rather, make references assuming the other characters — and the audiences watching — know what they mean. They substitute specificity with filler words like "stuff" and "things," and everyone understands the meaning. A particularly egregious example of Whedonspeak in *Redshirts* occurs after we're introduced to the microwave oven-like box, when an ensign, Collins, admits to Dahl that things aren't what they seem aboard the *Intrepid*:

> What are we going to say, Andy? . . . "Hi, welcome to the *Intrepid*, avoid the officers because it's likely you'll get killed if you're on an away team with them, and oh, by the way, here's a magic box we use for *impossible things*"? That would be a lovely first impression, wouldn't it?[5]

In a world in which ensigns feel powerless to change anything, sarcasm is their only weapon, and it's dished out in continual conversation. Dread, nostalgia, or sorrow might creep in if the dialogue stops.

I like to think of Whedonspeak as a language spoken by foreverized characters, that is, characters that are trapped in stories from which escape proves difficult. The best they can do is wink at the audience, letting us know that *they* know their context is fake and that, perhaps, some unseen force is influencing them to act according to a script or logic — but there might not be anything they (or we the readers) can do. Instead, they will remain forever present and forever conversing within a closed system without being able to change it.

Numerous superhero, sci-fi, and fantasy media incorporate Whedonspeak to enliven their dialogue: *The Avengers* and *Avengers: Age of Ultron* (both written and directed by Joss Whedon), the *Marvel's Avengers* video game, *Dungeons & Dragons: Honor Among Thieves*, and, perhaps infamously, Netflix's *Cowboy Bebop* reboot, to name only a few. (I'll delve into the *Cowboy Bebop* reboot in a later section.) Characters in these media don't just make quips about the events happening to them. They also just talk a lot, like the characters in *Redshirts*, because without explaining every detail about who is doing what, everyone but the diehard fans would be lost. Scriptwriters know that over-explaining motives and prior events helps fans remember why a plot is developing the way that it is and brings newbies up to speed. As a result, silence and contemplation are rare.

While characters in these films fill the silence with dialogue, fans do their part by continuing the conversation in real life. Fans not only consume their favorite media franchises but also talk about them on social media, host podcasts dissecting plot and character developments, and so forth. They do this to keep the intellectual property alive, and also to salute it as one would a flag or a leader — to honor the great works of the past as if it were one's duty. It might not register as work, but it is work nonetheless: a constant job of conversing.

"Repressive forces don't stop people expressing themselves," Deleuze said, "but rather force them to express themselves. What a relief to have nothing to say, the right to say nothing, because only then is there a chance of framing the rare, and ever rarer, thing that might be worth saying."[6] In other words, constant communication reduces the possibility of a meaningful point being made. And simply being able to converse with others all the time means nothing if we don't consider what we're communicating about and on whose terms. These are especially crucial points to consider when communicating on social platforms. The ability to engage constantly with others is one of social media's main attractions, yet free speech is not equally distributed online. A social platform is not a public space. There appears everywhere online the democratization of speaking one's voice, but doing so is always on the terms of the digital platform, which demands that users contribute so that data is produced for media corporations to better micro-target their ads at audiences for the next reboot.

A foreverized world seems to stretch without end. It is tiresome to live in one, to stand up and be counted as crew members, who are framed as disposable and subjected to violence, while leaders escape harm aboard a dangerous ship hurtling toward oblivion. We are encouraged to brand ourselves, to "sell" ourselves to companies, and as a result we are pressured to conform to inflexible roles, to perform as empty-headed sitcom people who never feel loss or pain, speaking to each other in the cynical language of Whedonspeak: aware of our fate but unable to do more than signal to others that we're aware. There is no time for nostalgia in a world like this, no tolerance for mourning loss or longing for stability. But loss comes for us all. It's not a matter of if, but when.

If Spring Will Ever Come

So far, I've examined how foreverism attempts to suppress nostalgia by keeping the past forever present. But coerced forgetting is just as anti-nostalgic as forced remembering, and can also aid in locking people into the present.

The horror of a world forced to live without a past appears in Yōko Ogawa's *The Memory Police*, published in 1994 and translated into English in 2019. In the novel, the inhabitants of an unnamed island slowly lose their memories as things around them disappear. The disappearances come unannounced. There is no grand declamation; the inhabitants merely awake one morning to suspect something has disappeared, and then, gradually, they realize what's missing. Any person found hiding a vanished object, like flowers, hats, or perfume, is disappeared by the Memory Police, an efficient, emotionless force in jackboots. The people of the island carry out the disappearances themselves not only because they

The disappearances affect labor on the island as well. Once hats disappear, milliners must learn to make umbrellas. Boat mechanics take jobs as security guards. When novels disappear, the narrator, a novelist herself, finds work as a typist for a spice company. Her production of words to create art is replaced with the gesture of typing copy. She goes from working on her novel at home to working in an office for ten hours a day, typing, filing, and answering the phone. Soon after starting the job, she finds it difficult to juggle work responsibilities with her home life.

Only in a world of forced disappearances would preservation be so prized. For those who can remember, the smallest object is precious. The narrator's editor, who goes by R, is one of the few on the island who never forgets, so the narrator decides to hide him from the Memory Police in a secret room in her house. The room is tiny, accessible by a trapdoor in the floor, with barely enough space for a narrow bed. There are no windows and no way to determine the time of day. It is a cell. Meanwhile, the Memory Police headquarters is lavish, with crystal chandeliers hanging from the ceiling, leather couches, and wall tapestries. The building seems untouched by the mass erasure of the island. As the novel unfolds, it is clear that either the Memory Police anticipate the disappearances and adapt in advance, or are allowed to retain the disappeared things.

The narrator fears that R's body is wasting away in the hidden room, but she wonders if that's the price one must pay to remember everything:

> Perhaps it was necessary to rid oneself of every-thing that was superfluous in order to immerse completely in this airless, soundproof, narrow space shrouded in the fear of discovery and arrest. In recompense for a mind that was able to retain everything, every memory, perhaps it was necessary that the body gradually fade away.[9]

Nothing can truly live in a preserved state forever, as R demonstrates. To preserve is by definition to freeze into rigor mortis. The living must adapt to survive in such a state, which is to say, they must learn to live as death. But is R freer in his cell than the islanders outside simply because he remembers? Or do the islanders enjoy a freedom denied to R? What is worse, to be a free amnesiac or a captive rememberer?

The more things disappear, the more the narrator wonders if the end is coming, if everything, including herself, will disappear. "End . . . conclusion . . . limit — how many times had I tried to imagine where I was headed, using words like these?" she asks.[10] The thought disturbs her. Time itself seems to have stopped. Winter drags on indefinitely. "We were entirely in the present," she realizes.[11]

She awakes one morning to find her left leg has disappeared. It is still there physically, but she has no memory of it and no knowledge of how to use it. The others on the island have forgotten their left legs as well. Then everyone's right arms disappear. Eventually their bodies disappear too, leaving nothing but voices. When this happens the Memory Police cease their enforcement. Finally the voices disappear. There is no one but R left, who remembers everything.

The Memory Police is a story about what happens when things don't end, when the present freezes and no temporal movement is allowed, no past and no future. Philosopher François J. Bonnet calls this privileging of the present "tautological living," which is always "plunging us into perpetual forgetting, saturated as we are with presentness."[12] He refers to tautological living as a "narcotic" because it "anaesthetizes any anguish we feel about the future that harbors our inevitable demise."[13] Its function is to fend off the creeping threat of death. Yet, as the narrator realizes in *The Memory Police*, the closer we get to achieving forever presence, the suspicion that we are approaching an end or limit grows stronger. Instead of distancing us from death, foreverizing the present immerses us in a void of death where nothing new grows. The past is either forgotten or it's not even the past anymore — it's the present.

Ogawa's novel doesn't merely suggest that losing things is devastating but also that our memories are shaped by things: flowers, clothing, even body parts. When these things disappear so do some of our memories. Although we don't have literal Memory Police enforcing mass forgetting in our world today, we do occasionally experience the shock of awaking in the morning to find that something very important, something precious and vital to life, has disappeared. And perhaps we've thrown it away, seeing it as useless, afraid we might not otherwise survive. But these objects may hold information that can only be accessed by incorporating them in our lives. Consider the outdated media so often framed as unenduring — fading Polaroids, tape cassettes, floppy disks, and more — these too might contain truths that are erased during digitization. They might be truths that can only be discovered by interacting with the idiosyncrasies of the media, by seeing the fade of the photograph, hearing the warp of the tape, holding the disk in your hand. These sensory elements, these aesthetics of patination, produce their own meanings in the same way that the World War I footage that Peter Jackson restored communicated meanings about the past that were lost in restoration.

Faye Valentine's Tape

The potential for obsolete media to produce their own meanings is explored in a classic series that was subjected to its own bit of foreverizing in 2021: *Cowboy Bebop*, a futuristic space epic from the late 1990s, widely regarded as one of the greatest anime of all time. In the eighteenth episode, "Speak Like a Child," Spike and Jet, bounty hunters aboard the *Bebop* spaceship, receive a Betamax tape in the mail and embark on a quest to find a working deck to watch it. They travel to Earth in search of an abandoned museum where the last known Beta player sits gathering dust. They rappel down an elevator shaft twenty-eight floors, crawl through flooded ducts, climb down rusting ladders, and inch across pipes until they reach a room filled with aging tape players. They grab a television and what they think is a Beta deck and make their way back. Turns out they've accidentally taken a VCR, which isn't compatible with Betamax. Exhausted, they set their analog cargo aside and try to forget about the whole diversion, until a package containing a Betamax player mysteriously arrives.

Faye Valentine, the amnesiac bounty hunter wanted for her outstanding debts, arrives back at the ship as Spike and Jet load the Beta tape into the player. The crew is stunned to see on the flickering screen a young Faye with her childhood friends. The tape, it turns out, is a time capsule message from Faye's younger self to be played ten years in the future.

Born in the twentieth century, Faye was cryogenically frozen for over fifty years after a space shuttle accident in the early twenty-first century. During her slumber a cataclysm destroys much of the Earth, wiping out nearly all records, including any information about herself. When she awakens she finds herself in a strange future world with a new name and an unpayable bill for the medical procedure that saved her life.

Where the revived Faye is cynical and skeptical of others, the young Faye on the tape is hopeful and shy. In her recorded message to her future self, the young Faye cheers, "Do your best! Do your best! Don't lose me!" Faye watches in horror as she cannot remember the person on the screen. "In your time, I'm no longer here," she says on the tape, "but I am here today. And I'll always be cheering for you, right here. Cheering for you, my only self."[14] Imploring herself not to change, the younger Faye is unrecognizable to the present Faye.

The Betamax was a dead medium by the time *Cowboy Bebop* aired. The VHS won the videotape format war and became the standard tape for several decades, until it too was replaced by other media. The Betamax didn't survive, and yet, in the episode, it does. It remembers. It's Faye who doesn't remember and who, after watching the tape and driven by a nostalgia for a time she doesn't recall, eventually goes searching for home in a later episode only to find it gone. She struggles to accept this tragic fate, the knowledge learned from so many nostalgic sojourns. But unlike other nostalgic subjects, Faye doesn't fully know what she misses, for the cryogenicists stole her memory. The debt agency, however, remembers: it tethers her to the only identity it cares about, the one that owes money.

There are versions of ourselves traced onto dying media, somewhere. Memories captured on tape, in photographs, on fading screens. Perhaps they will wend their way to us at some point. Will we recognize the person on the screen, in the image, on tape? Even if our moments are recorded, and framed as memories, that doesn't mean we'll be able to recognize our younger selves in the future. We too may have our memories erased by outside forces, dogged by new technologies of control, like Faye. She suffers the loss of her data and, therefore, loses herself. And she is billed for what was done without her consent to keep her preserved and to one day revitalize her. The cost is her memory.

Interacting with obsolete media, such as Betamax tapes, can be an eerie experience, especially when they subvert the expectation that they don't last. Perhaps it is the digital, often framed as infallible, that won't last. Data centers promise to foreverize our memories, but their precarity all but guarantees data loss. Up until 2019, the US nuclear command and control system ran on floppy disks. The transition to digital storage was lauded as an overdue step forward, but now the system is more vulnerable to hacking than it was when it relied on floppy disks, which aren't connected to the Internet.[15] Maybe the outdatedness of older technologies is what makes them valuable, in terms of security and memory. Maybe there are keys to the truth of the past encoded onto the obsolete technologies waiting in the dusty depths. And it might take a risky dive down through the wreckage for us to find them.

We never really know who sent the tape and the player to the *Bebop* ship. We can guess it was Faye who sent it to her future self, a memento she doesn't understand, an attempt to foreverize herself and maybe prevent future nostalgia. Like the rest of the series, "Speak Like a Child" explores timeless themes about the human condition, and through Faye's backstory, it ponders certain questions about memory and power. Who benefits from preservation, and who suffers? Could a dead medium remember the past more clearly than a network designed to keep track of you?

In 2021 Netflix attempted to foreverize Faye and the rest of the *Bebop* crew by releasing a live-action reboot of the series. Netflix, like so many media corporations today, produces content by foreverizing the intellectual properties of yesterday, but it failed in its attempt and therefore couldn't cure the nostalgia for the original anime. Critics and the public excoriated the reboot for lacking the nuance and artistry of the original. It was also criticized for its excessive usage of Whedonspeak, like when Faye is handcuffed to a toilet by Jet and Spike shortly after meeting them in the first episode. She says, "Hey dick-hole! Super cool accommodations, but do you think you could handcuff me to an even bigger, more disgusting toilet? 'Cause that would be great."[16]

The original anime relied on musical montages, shared glances, and atmosphere to communicate all that needed to be said. It also explored the horror of being chained to your past, confined to a role you didn't sign up for, as did *Redshirts*. But unlike John Scalzi's novel, the original *Cowboy Bebop* makes a more compelling critique of foreverism in "Speak Like a Child." And it does so without any Whedonspeak.

The *Bebop* reboot's reliance on Whedonspeak isn't simply an attempt to meet contemporary dialogue standards set in place by Joss Whedon and other writers of his ilk. As I mentioned previously, it's also the language of foreverized content, a style spoken by characters who can never disappear or die and who can never react to situations with sincere emotions such as nostalgia or sorrow. They are to remain trapped within a static universe by a media conglomerate promising wealth and fame to the human actors willing to portray them. If the original *Cowboy Bebop* is a story about characters haunted by their pasts, the Netflix reboot is about those same characters haunted by the original anime. Watching it is a surreal experience: it's as if the actors playing in the reboot know that they're in a reboot. You can almost see it in their eyes, the recognition that they're acting within a closed system, puppeteered by some unseen hand.

In the world outside the reboot many try to escape their past, while powerful forces conspire to lock them in place forever, because there is an incentive to keep people in unchanging roles.

The incentive is greater than merely an assault on the nostalgia that follows change. Branded, legible selves are important to capital. So are working bodies. If nostalgic quests to restore the past generate labor for capitalism, then they are permitted, encouraged even — especially if the restored past is profitable in the present. Otherwise, an amnesiac might be desired, someone whose real past can be erased and replaced with a tracking device, someone burdened by debt and blocked from moving forward. But memories aren't so easily erased. They might show up at our doorstep unannounced.

4

Now And Forever

Investigative journalist Jim Hougan is most famous for his 1984 book, *Secret Agenda: Watergate, Deep Throat, and the CIA*, which presented new evidence, obtained via a Freedom of Information Act Request, challenging the "received version" of the Watergate scandal. But in the mid-1970s he wrote a book called *Decadence: Radical Nostalgia, Narcissism, and Decline in the Seventies* and made this prediction:

> There is no reason to expect that the mass of Americans will experience a revolutionary Nostalgia. . . . Indeed, the idea is ludicrous. What would it be like? One imagines millions of Americans . . . marching down Pennsylvania Avenue chanting:

BRING / BACK / THE GOOD OLD DAYS!
BRING / BACK / THE GOOD OLD DAYS!
BRING / BACK / THE GOOD OLD DAYS![1]

Forty years later Donald Trump registered the phrase "Make America Great Again" with the US Patent and Trademark Office. It quickly appeared on billboards, red baseball caps, and T-shirts. It went viral on social media. And when Trump lost his presidential reelection bid to Joe Biden in November 2020, thousands did march down Pennsylvania Avenue, though they didn't chant "Bring back the good old days" — they chanted "Make America great again." His supporters chanted it again on January 6, 2021, as they marched down Pennsylvania Avenue once more and besieged the US Capitol in an attempt to overturn the result of the election by force.

Hougan's words seem unfamiliar to us now. Nostalgia can be, and has been, used to advance political interests. But in 1975 he couldn't imagine that anyone would see a potential for action in nostalgia because, he wrote, "Americans would first have to recognize the depth of their loss" — which he didn't see them capable of doing.[2] He called nostalgia "no more authentic than a hooker's love" and mourned the suffocation of progress at the hands of such an infantile, regressive sentiment.[3] Nostalgia was a lie, he argued, an emotion that fabricated memories to keep us cozy in the alienated present, and it was surely ineffective at uniting groups of people to act: "It is much more likely that the emotion will decay into a pervasive wistfulness that falsifies the past and serves, not as a lever in the present, but as an escape from it."[4]

The retro sitcom *Happy Days* might have had Americans rocking around the clock in 1975, but plenty of others shared Hougan's negative opinion of nostalgia. While he considered it politically impotent, the top brass of the US military had long thought of nostalgia as rather unpatriotic, perhaps even a national security concern, an opinion dating as far back as the Civil War, when J. Theodore Calhoun presented his paper discriminating against soldiers from rural backgrounds. After World War II, the US military worried that communists might employ nostalgic propaganda to entice soldiers to defect or weaken their will to fight. In 1954, the Department of the Army issued a pamphlet listing methods that could be used to induce nostalgia in homesick soldiers in the

Korean War. It fretfully described North Korean leaflets depicting a young American woman waking up next to her husband; the pamphlet urged soldiers in future conflicts to remember their duty to their country instead of their wives back home.[5] There were anxieties that enemy units might resort to extreme psychological measures. They might broadcast familiar songs over loudspeakers on the battlefield to exploit the nostalgia of soldiers, which could drive them to commit sabotage to hasten their return home. Or soldiers might hand themselves over for capture voluntarily, so that they can escape fighting and live long enough to see their home after the war. In other words, one could be so nostalgic for one's country that one might willingly become a prisoner of war for it.[6]

Other denigrations of nostalgia followed. Under-secretary of State George W. Ball delivered an address in March 1965, later published as a pamphlet titled "The Dangers of Nostalgia." He stressed that "after almost every great period in human endeavor, there comes a time when people begin to look backward with a warm glow and to feel that heroic exertions are no longer required." But he warned that nostalgia for a prewar era was "a dangerous mistake" and maintained that, even though some might think the world wars are over, that doesn't mean the US must practice isolationism. The world is too complex, he said, for nostalgia, and the US must never "withdraw ... from a high measure of responsibility for the maintenance of order and stability through the free world." It was a call for US expansionism, for the US to act as the world's police, and for Americans not to "turn [their] backs on the world as it was — and wish it were something different."[7]

By 1975, however, faith in progress was declining, and the past looked increasingly appealing. And by the time Donald Trump announced his run for president in 2015, people everywhere recognized that something had changed, that things had been lost, and they wanted to get back to the good old days, when everything was right and whole.

Nostalgia's rebirth as a political cudgel didn't happen accidentally. It was midwifed by a handful of powerful influencers who connivingly framed the present as irretrievably lost and charged specific groups of people with the crime. Donald Trump was merely one of these influencers.

During his presidential tenure he blamed immigrants, LGBTQ+ persons, people of color, and the entire Democratic Party for weakening the power of white Americans. According to Trump, white men in particular had lost it all: their jobs, traditions, heritage, and, perhaps worst of all, their history. And he vowed to restore what was supposedly taken from them.

Over a half-century ago, the US was afraid that a homesick citizenry would keep the country stuck in the past. It is now afraid of what might happen if the country doesn't return to the past. This shift in attitude amounts to a change in nostalgia's utility to capitalism. If inflamed emotions, including nostalgia, could produce labor, then a controlled emotional burn might be profitable to powerful elites, who could masquerade as emotional stewards guiding the public to a state of exploitable passion.

Putting Nostalgia to Work

Political leaders today routinely invoke nostalgia in their rhetoric — not to invite the public to bask in a yearning glow, to pause in reflection, but to do the work the leader says is needed to revive the past and keep it forever present. The political weaponization of nostalgia is a softer, less punitive (but no less dangerous) method for stopping nostalgic spread: frame the past as a lost cause, suggest your political platform is the solution to reviving it, and then put the public to work.

The process to foreverize a nation might proceed like this. It might begin with a call to restore the past: a nostalgic seed is planted, perhaps by a political candidate hoping to capitalize on the action tendencies of the emotion (its past-gazing, misremembering, bittersweet tendencies). Their order is to remember those fond days, the world of yesteryear. But because nostalgia can inspire idleness, some might waste time dreaming of the past instead of working. Reminiscing on its own isn't enough. To restore the lost utopia requires labor, productivity, and consumption. If one can convince the public to work towards their nostalgic desire, then perhaps that work can be commodified, the emotional equivalent of carbon capture. In the end, profits are generated and nostalgia is extinguished. Or so they think.

There is also a chain of command here. The political candidate, like any nostalgic elite, reminisces and plans to restore things while the laborers do the work needed to restore. What the restorers find is that the past rebooted into the present isn't quite the same as it was. It looks different, doesn't quite smell the same. It sounds like an aging band reunited: a bit rusty, not quite as good. The work to restore the past also produces emotional fallout in the form of anger and frustration. The past wears its patina so thick, it is so hard to scrub off. It takes time and effort to restore, and one might grow irritable trying to do it. And if the pressure to restore is high, that too produces frustration because, according to our nostalgic leaders, the very future might depend on this restoring.

But restoring the past isn't nearly enough. There must be some guarantee it can persist into the future; it must be future-proof, like an electric vehicle with a retro design. Beyond the labor needed to advance a nostalgic political campaign — the graphic design of logos, the production of yard signs, the drafting of talking points to be aired on cable news, the canvassing to get out the vote — there is also the work of sharing those talking points with others on social media, the endless posting of political memes, the very act of watching news programs and reading opinion pieces lamenting the lost causes the candidate promises to restore. This is the "forever conversing" part of political foreverism.

Jim Hougan wrote that Americans would have to recognize the depth of their loss before they could experience a revolutionary nostalgia. For decades now, far right political leaders, in particular, have successfully induced such a recognition in certain groups. But they aren't content with the occasional nostalgia for the past — with allowing those feelings to merely come and go. Instead, they will promise to heal nostalgia by first convincing their supporters that they've had everything taken from them, and then by vowing to return to them what was lost. They will inflame nostalgic sentiments with discriminatory rhetoric that frames the past as perfect, and then calm them down by scapegoating marginalized groups who are often accused of ruining the present. The danger of these nostalgic appeals isn't merely that they suggest the past used to be great, but that they imply the far right is the only political movement that can return the country to greatness. Like the foreverizing of entertainment media, the political foreverizing espoused by the far right aims to future-proof a version of the past that only serves the powerful few.

Missing the Past

"We have been prohibited from living with nostalgia, melancholy, and the fear of death," François J. Bonnet argues in *After Death*. "They have been banished from the empire of the present."[8] From political leaders to media corporations, major voices today are suggesting that living with nostalgia — not trying to suppress it, not attempting a return to the past, just simply living with it — is abnormal. They are no different today than the positivists discussed earlier. Their mission is to produce an eternal present. "Eternity is the present without shadows," Bonnet writes. "An instantaneous, tautological, endlessly renewed present. A static time in which nothing can happen."[9] In a foreverized society, loss, including the ultimate loss of death, is a condition that darkens the smile of the self-actualized man, who advocates for living in the present. Such an existence is a weary one, caffeinated and wide awake, plugged into news and with an opinion on every remote event. Nostalgia has no place among the self-actualized. Rather, as Bonnet notes, nostalgia "leads us elsewhere. And elsewhere hardly exists anymore."[10]

In terms of foreverism, death is a problem to be solved, and increasingly tech corporations position themselves as competent problem solvers. To solve death, they first reduce life to data and then promise the public the application, and animation, of data using artificial intelligence. It is a mission to achieve the formula Herman Melville composed for immortality so long ago: "for immortality is but ubiquity in time."[11]

Here, the logic of the reboot is applied to human life: a deceased person can live on through a technological medium. Amazon followed this logic when it demonstrated that its Alexa voice assistant could replicate human voices, but even that wasn't a sufficient display of AI prowess. The megacorporation then claimed that Alexa could speak in the voice of a deceased loved one. Before a crowd at one of the company's AI conferences, Rohit Prasad, an Amazon scientist, remarked, in a blatant appeal to foreverizing, "While AI can't eliminate that pain of loss, it can definitely make their memories last." He rolls a video of a young boy in his bedroom asking his Kids Edition

Amazon Echo Dot, with its panda face printed on the speaker, "Alexa, can grandma finish reading me *The Wizard of Oz*?" Alexa responds, "Okay," and a synthetic voice mimicking the grandmother's reads from the L. Frank Baum classic while the boy happily follows along.[12]

Prasad's point was that Amazon can enrich our "lasting personal relationships" by using less than a minute of recorded audio to mimic the voice of another person. The fact that it was the voice of a dead relative merely reinforced Amazon's foreverizing obsessions: it regards its technologies as possible solutions to the problem of death. But Amazon isn't the only tech company with such arrogant ambitions. Google, social media platforms, Apple, and the rest of Big Tech promote constant engagement; to keep the conversation going, to keep scrolling and posting, is to interact meaningfully with others. They cannot bear the thought of a lapse in engagement, so when a person dies, the data can't just be preserved, it must speak too. We are told that data ought to continue interacting with us, eliding the meaning of the living and the dead into so much information to be extracted and sold to advertisers. Like all forms of foreverizing, the purpose of voice replication is to eliminate nostalgic feelings, but the boy's grandmother in Amazon's promo video isn't actually speaking to him from inside the smart speaker. She is a surrogate cobbled together from data. And in all likelihood, listening to the surrogate speak wouldn't soothe the boy but, rather, inflame his longing for her.

Could it be that instead of seeing nostalgia as a disease to be cured, as so many positivists and physicians through the nineteenth and early twentieth centuries thought, we view it as an emotion to be managed like any other? Instead of suppressing the emotion to stop it, or trying to relieve it through either the consumption of retro or by voting for political candidates who promise to revive the past, perhaps we ought to reappraise it. We might ask ourselves what the short- and long-term consequences of feeling nostalgic are in a given situation. Will it prove beneficial for us to relieve our nostalgia by indulging in the past? Or does our nostalgia provide us with some truth that is crucial for us to understand the present and the future? And will suppressing it or running headlong back into the past to make the feeling go away actually destroy that truth?

History, as always, provides possible answers. While others were busy denigrating nostalgia, as I discussed in Chapter 1, not every physician in the nineteenth century agreed that it was pathological. Some weren't so sure that it should be cured at all. Already in 1830 the physician Hyacinthe Musset had asked, "Should one try to smother this sweet sentiment which makes us cherish with such tenderness our family, our friends, and the places where we have been born?" He pointed out that the "cure" for nostalgia might be too horrible to imagine, that it might mutilate humanity.[13]

Over a hundred years later, the psychoanalyst Alexander R. Martin wrote that suppressing emotions, including nostalgia, was indeed harmful. People were going to feel nostalgic in stressful contexts. That doesn't mean they're going to resort to murder or arson, but they might long for stability — and that's completely normal. Martin was addressing the nostalgia of soldiers particularly. Instead of laughing the nostalgia out of soldiers, he urged military leaders to let them express their homesick emotions. "If . . . homesickness is repressed," he wrote, "then even greater loneliness descends upon the individual. . . . The world loses its meaning. What revival of the past makes people happy, so therefore the past should be revived. But just because Disney, Paramount Global, or Amazon might suggest that a rebooted classic will make us happy doesn't mean it will or, if it will, whether that's a good thing. Could it be that audiences love older music, movies, television series, books, and other media simply because they aren't produced anymore? Could it be our nostalgia for old media is the reason we enjoy consuming them and that the more companies try to foreverize the intellectual properties of the past, the less we might love them?

Sometimes companies justify foreverizing by acknowledging that some timeless classics include remarks that were unchallenged in their own time but are insensitive today. To honor the classics and respect present-day standards of decency, alterations to the original text are proposed. Works from authors such as Agatha Christie, Ian Fleming, and Roald Dahl are being revised to remove offensive language, which has prompted accusations of censorship and opened up discussions about which classics should be edited and which elements removed.

This process of retroactive editing has been going on in the entertainment industry for quite that's what everybody is going to remember. The other versions will disappear. Even the 35 million tapes of *Star Wars* out there won't last more than 30 or 40 years. A hundred years from now, the only version of the movie that anyone will remember will be the DVD version [of the Special Edition], and you'll be able to project it on a 20' by 40' screen with perfect quality.[17]

For Lucas, artists have the right to constantly update their art. When is a work of art ever finished then? When will the *Star Wars* universe undergo its own big crunch? Speaking specifically about cinema, Lucas has an answer: "In essence, films never get finished, they get abandoned."[18]

In a time of widespread foreverizing, when major works of art are always being tweaked, it's worth considering which classics should be abandoned or, at the very least, finished. For some, including George Lucas, this amounts to artistic heresy. It would also mean the category of "classic" would likely disappear because most classics are always being updated to meet the needs of the present. Classics really can't be "timeless" without undergoing some kind of foreverization, without being updated to account for changing standards and norms through remastering, re-editing, remixing, and so forth. Without routine foreverizing, some classics would probably be forgotten. Maybe that's a good thing. But that would challenge the rampant belief that classics are permanent and immutable and that proving otherwise offends some sense of the past as great and able to withstand the changes of time.

Like the older atavistic discourses, foreverism frames the problematic aspects of the past — its nightmarish realities unforgotten by so many — as throwback traits that have been bred out. Now you can consume the past without worrying that you might be ignoring the injustices of history. But foreverizing isn't as progressive a measure as we might think. Altering the original content of texts doesn't amount to much progress if their stories bolster the same norms of familialism, militarism, patriarchy, productivity, and nationalism. To foreverize something is to make small upgrades constantly within a closed system. It's like updating your smartphone software: there are negligible changes, but you're still using a smartphone owned by the same company that developed the software. Those elements won't change even though the software has been updated. The same logic applies to foreverizing older texts with offensive language: some words might change, and the content might be so offensive, so heinous, that the change is justified. But the story remains basically the same. In fact, retaining the storyline is a priority when companies remove insensitive content from older books and movies. The process is explicitly about keeping the overarching narrative intact while making small upgrades to keep it up to date in the present.

But why should we rely on older stories to make judgments about the present? Why not just write new stories with new characters? For one thing, media companies aren't interested in new content. They're comfortable betting on pre-existing intellectual properties, hoping to make enormous profits on recognizable brands to maintain their profitability forever, to render franchises contextless to appeal to as many people as possible. When Agatha Christie's great-grandson James Prichard, who is also the CEO of the company that licenses Christie's rights, was asked about the decision to revise Christie's novels to meet current norms, he admitted as much: "My great-grandmother would not have wanted to offend anyone. I don't believe we need to leave what I would term offensive language in our books, because frankly all I care about is that people can enjoy Agatha Christie stories forever."[19]

Both the updating of classic texts and the reactions against such updating signal a desire to keep the classics alive in the present. We might, instead, accept that some works are just more timeless than others, and the ones that aren't might need to be forgotten. The works that need a foreverized makeover to remain timeless really have one main purpose anyway: to reassure audiences that they didn't miss the artistic achievements of the past and they won't miss them ever again. And yet, most foreverized content seems incapable of measuring up to the truly timeless classics. It is the great irony of foreverism that, by keeping the past forever present, it continues to assert the primacy of the past.

I am reminded of a moment from a few years ago. A colleague of mine at the university where I teach referenced the American sitcom *Friends* in a class of undergraduates. "But you probably don't remember that show," he remarked. Murmurs of shock rippled through the audience of nearly one hundred students. "Yes we do! Yes we do!"

they shouted back, assuring my surprised colleague that they'd binge-watched every episode.
They were offended, but more than anything,
they appeared panicked. Their adamant cries gave
away a latent fear that they were born too late and
had missed the great cultural moments of history, and now there were none left. Foreverism
seeks to silence those anxieties by rebooting the
"great" moments from the past that we might
have missed, with the hope that we might not
miss another. Otherwise, if you don't know the
classics then you might be left behind, locked out
of time in some waiting room forever, counting
the days until the coast cities submerge under-
water, measuring time by software updates only.

The Future of Foreverism

A few months after the "Foreverism" briefing,
TrendWatching published its companion docu-
ment, "NOWISM: Why Currency Is the New
Currency," and outlined its foundations:

Consumers' ingrained lust for instant gratification is being satisfied by a host of novel, important
(offline and online) real-time products, services

and experiences. Consumers are also feverishly contributing to the real-time content avalanche that's building as we speak. As a result, expect your brand and company to have no choice but to finally mirror and join the "now," in all its splendid chaos, realness and excitement.[20]

The briefing claimed that the causes of nowism are the "age of abundance," the "focus on consuming experiences," and "instant gratification" in the online world. Examples of nowist developments are pop-up shops, "infolust" (defined as "lusting after knowing what friends, family, celebs, colleagues, foes and so on, are doing/saying/thinking right now"), experiencing "raw" events like live concerts and public controversies, and "urge alerts ... aimed at stimulating impulse buys," like when a company drops a limited run of clothing or a local bakery announces freshly baked goods.[21] But none of these points stunned me more than when, halfway down the document, I came across a picture of Zygmunt Bauman, the late sociologist and critic of consumerism.

In a truly surreal section, the briefing recommends learning more about nowism by reading

Bauman's classic book *Liquid Modernity*, and even offers a summary:

> "Liquid Modernity" is Bauman's term for the present condition of the world as contrasted with the "solid" modernity that preceded it. . . . Social forms and institutions no longer have enough time to solidify and cannot serve as frames of reference for human actions and long-term life plans, so individuals have to find other ways to organize their lives. Individuals have to splice together an unending series of short-term projects and episodes that don't add up to the kind of sequence to which concepts like "career" and "progress" could be meaningfully applied. Such fragmented lives require individuals to be flexible and adaptable — to be constantly ready and willing to change tactics at short notice, to abandon commitments and loyalties without regret and to pursue opportunities according to their current availability. In liquid modernity the individual must act, plan actions and calculate the likely gains and losses of acting (or failing to act) under conditions of endemic uncertainty.[22]

Right below the excerpt is a space in the briefing to enter your email address so that you'll

"Never miss a Trend Briefing again." The fact that this invitation seemed to prove Bauman's point about acting "under conditions of endemic uncertainty" was apparently lost on the authors of the briefing.

It's clear that the marketing industry has become something like a theorist, albeit one that composes theory to grease the wheels of corporate capitalism. (TrendWatching even admits it's writing something like theory. After the Bauman section, the publication notes, "Enough theory . . . let's get organized." It then proceeds to explain the nowist developments that I mentioned earlier.) Some of this "theory" amounts to little more than indiscriminate concept generation, cranking out terms like "infolust," "hypertasking," and "snackonomy" that might not prove useful outside the realm of marketing, or at all. Other terms might actually be more heuristic than others. But when a trend firm cites Zygmunt Bauman to support its flimsy theorizing, and especially when the passage cited so clearly describes conditions of oppression that the marketing world views as conditions of possibility, it is time, I think, to take the theorizing seriously. We critics and theorists, readers and writers alike — all who desire to change this unequal world in the name of social justice — need to reckon with the theories about consumer capitalism being espoused by consumer capitalism itself.

I have attempted to take foreverism seriously in this book. Perhaps I am merely contributing another -ism to the concept mill. I'll let the reader decide. But to me, both foreverism and nowism are more than just throwaway terms to add to the pile of clickbait concepts proliferating online today. They successfully describe key developments in the digital age: the persistent focus on keeping everything present, either in a series of present moments one after another (nowism) or an elongated present that extends forever and swallows up the past and future (foreverism).

To resist foreverism, we need to first recognize it. It might seem challenging if we're accustomed to using the word *nostalgia* to describe the latest reboot or classic rock reunion tour. But instead of accusing the next nineties throwback flick of "nostalgia," we might ask: is anyone actually nostalgic for this? Or is the production company or streaming platform assuming we are and providing us with what they think we're longing for?

Is the point to keep the past present so that we aren't nostalgic for it anymore?

As I've mentioned throughout this book, nostalgia can't be easily extinguished. Surrounded by retro fashion, music, and entertainment, one might still yearn for the past. This is a fundamental truth of nostalgia: we can't relive the past, so there is always the possibility we'll miss it — even in a world where older cultural works are constantly being rebooted, even when we have the past at our fingertips. The emotion can't be disciplined out of us, and we can't consume our way out of it. In truth, nostalgia is an emotion that aids in the production and reinterpretation of memory. We really can't form some of our memories without it.

Future studies of foreverism might explore other emotions that are suppressed beneath the demands to stay forever present, forever beta, and forever conversing — like relief, contentment, hope, boredom, sorrow, even happiness, the emotion foreverism tries to deliver in spades. As with nostalgia, these targeted emotions aren't fully suppressed. By targeting them, foreverism inadvertently produces them among the public.

As emotions threaten the reactionaries' definition of a "civilized" public, more intimidating efforts to quell dissent will follow on the argument that emotional displays that challenge capitalist demands weaken law and order, and must therefore be punished. In an attempt to straighten out an emotional public, reactionaries will often promise to relieve nostalgia through the circulation of resentful, prejudicial discourses. These include revanchist missions to protect nation-states from suspicious "outsiders," as well as replacement theories that claim that white citizens are slowly being replaced by immigrants of color and a decline in white births. The disseminators of these discourses will first posit that there once was a white kingdom, rich in normative traditions, that has been stolen by intruders. They will then offer a curative to revive the kingdom and advance their campaign to try and prevent the disappearance of white men.

It's time we recognize that these discourses are actively attempting to suppress the emotions that threaten the systems of oppression under capitalism. A political appeal to the "good old days" or a social media account posting throwback clips might not seem like they're trying to quash

Notes

Chapter 1: When Nothing Ever Ends

1 Hans Gross, *Criminal Psychology: A Manual for Judges, Practitioners, and Students*, trans. Horace M. Kallen (Boston: Little, Brown, 1918), 77–78.

2 Willis H. McCann, "Nostalgia: A Review of the Literature," *Psychological Bulletin* 38 (1941): 167.

3 Ibid., 168.

4 Ernst Kretschmer, *A Text-Book of Medical Psychology*, trans. E. B. Strauss (Oxford: Oxford University Press, 1934), 187.

5 Edmund S. Conklin, *Principles of Adolescent Psychology* (New York: Henry Holt, 1935), 209–16.

6 McCann, "Nostalgia: A Review," 168.

7 J. Theodore Calhoun, "Nostalgia as a Disease of Field Service," *Medical & Surgical Reporter* 11, no. 9 (February 27, 1864): 130–32. Reprinted in *Journal of Civil War Medicine* 22, no. 2 (2018): 56–58.

8 Medical Society of the Second Division, Third Corps, Army of the Potomac, "Discussion on Nostalgia," *Medical and Surgical Reporter* 11, no. 10 (March 5, 1864): 150–52. Reprinted in *Journal of Civil War Medicine* 22, no. 2 (2018): 58–61.

9 L.W. Kline, "The Migratory Impulse vs. Love of Home," *The American Journal of Psychology* 10, no. 1 (1898): 81.

10 Michel Foucault, "22 January 1975," *Abnormal: Lectures at the Collège de France 1974–1975*, ed. Arnold I. Davidson, trans. Graham Burchell (London: Picador, 2003), 57–58.

11 Steve Harvey, "Passion for the Past: Nostalgia Marketing and the Retro Revolution," Fabrik Brands, https://fabrikbrands.com/nostalgia-marketing/

12 Donald W. Hendon, "Bicentennials Come and Go, but the Nostalgia Market Is Here to Stay, Perhaps in a Product Life Cycle 'Pigtail'," *Marketing News* (July 4, 1975): 7.

13 George Rosen, "Nostalgia: A 'Forgotten' Psychological Disorder," *Psychological Medicine* 5, no. 4 (November 1975): 340–54.

14 *The Mary Tyler Moore Show*, "I Was a Single for WJM," CBS (March 2, 1974).

15 Michael S. Roth, "Dying of the Past: Medical Studies of Nostalgia in Nineteenth-Century France," *History and Memory* 3, no. 1 (1991): 19.

16 CBS News, "Read the full transcript of the South Carolina Democratic debate" (February 25, 2020), https://www.cbsnews.com/news/south-carolina-democratic-debate-full-transcript-text/

17 iMemories website, "About Us," https://www.imemo
   ries.com/about
18 "Foreverism: Consumers and businesses embracing
   conversations, lifestyles and products that are 'never
   done,'" TrendWatching (2009), https://www.trendwa
   tching.com/trends/foreverism
19 Ibid.
20 Ibid.
21 Ibid.

Chapter 2: Everything Not Saved Will Be Lost

1 Nancy Martha West, *Kodak and the Lens of
   Nostalgia* (Charlottesville: University Press of Virginia,
   2000), 4.
2 Svetlana Boym, *The Future of Nostalgia* (New York:
   Basic Books, 2001), 15.
3 Mark Fisher, *Capitalist Realism: Is There No Alternative?*
   (Winchester, UK: Zero Books, 2009), 3.
4 Matt Soergel, "Jacksonville icon reflects on recording
   Lynyrd Skynyd's first songs, including 'Free Bird',"
   The Florida Times-Union (October 23, 2020), https://
   www.jacksonville.com/story/entertainment/music/20
   20/10/23/jacksonville-icon-reflects-recording-lynyrd
   -skynyrds-first-songs/3713009001/
5 TOTEM website, "About," https://www.totemmx
   .com/about
6 Anthony Breznican, "*Star Wars* Forever: How Kathleen
   Kennedy Is Expanding the Galaxy," *Vanity Fair* (May
   18, 2022), https://www.vanityfair.com/hollywood/20
   22/05/star-wars-kathleen-kennedy

7 Alexandra Fiorentino-Swinton, "Nostalgia for Nostalgia," *Real Life* (January 6, 2022), https://realli femag.com/nostalgia-for-nostalgia/

8 Ibid.

9 Abe Beame, "The Follow: A. S. Hamrah, Critic," Passion of the Weiss (May 24, 2022), https://www.passion weiss.com/2022/05/24/the-follow-a-s-hamrah-critic/

10 Talia Soghomonian, "Ian McKellen: 'Filming 'The Hobbit' made me cry with frustration,'" *NME* (November 17, 2012), https://www.nme.com/news/ film/ian-mckellen-filming-the-hobbit-made-me-cry -with-f-877575

11 Phil de Semlyen, "Ian McKellen on coming out in Hollywood, 'The Hobbit' and not being Dumbledore," *Time Out* (May 22, 2018), https://www.timeout.com /film/ian-mckellen-on-coming-out-in-hollywood-the -hobbit-and-not-being-dumbledore

12 The Howard Stern Show, "Jake Gyllenhaal Forgot His Lines While Filming 'Spider-Man: Far From Home'," YouTube video, 3:27 (October 5, 2021), https://www .youtube.com/watch?v=aKAp3q6Bv8w&ab_channel= TheHowardSternShow

13 Peter Bradshaw, "*They Shall Not Grow Old* review – Peter Jackson's electrifying journey into the First World War trenches," *The Guardian* (October 16, 2018), https://www.theguardian.com/film/2018/oct/16 /they-shall-not-grow-old-review-first-world-war-peter -jackson

14 Luke McKernan, "Colouring the Past," Luke McKernan blog (January 25, 2018), https://lukemcker nan.com/2018/01/25/colouring-the-past/

15   Breznican, "*Star Wars* Forever."

16   Anna Nicolaou & Antoine Gara, "Song Lyrics Strike a Chord with Private Equity," *Financial Times* (October 27, 2021), https://www.ft.com/content/83753cb0-0007-4420-a9a9-99a3b9b72778. See also Grafton Tanner, "Yesterday Once More," *Real Life* (November 22, 2021), https://reallifemag.com/yesterday-once-more/ and Rich Woodall, "Mass Hipgnosis," *The Baffler* (March 15, 2021), https://thebaffler.com/latest/mass-hipgnosis-woodall

17   Double Down News, "How Smoked Salmon Is Destroying Our Minds | George Monbiot," YouTube video, 8:28 (March 25, 2021), https://www.youtube.com/watch?v=JsSF1_TYdWw&ab_channel=DoubleDownNews

18   Juliane Gluge, et al, "An overview of the uses of per- and polyfluoroalkyl substances (PFAS)," *Environmental Sciences: Processes and Impacts*, no. 12 (2020), 2345–73.

19   iMemories home page, https://www.imemories.com/

20   Mél Hogan, "Facebook Data Storage Centers as the Archive's Underbelly," *Television & New Media*, vol. 16, no. 1 (2015): 5.

21   Ibid., 8–9.

22   Ibid., 9.

23   Laurel Wamsley, "Library of Congress Will No Longer Archive Every Tweet," NPR (December 26, 2017), https://www.npr.org/sections/thetwo-way/2017/12/26/573609499/library-of-congress-will-no-longer-archive-every-tweet

24   Hogan, "Facebook Data Storage," 9.

25 David Renshaw, "MySpace confirms 12 years of music lost in 'server migration'," *The Fader* (March 18, 2019), https://www.thefader.com/2019/03/18/myspace-server -migration-loss-music

26 Jay Greene, "Amazon's cloud-computing outage on Wednesday was triggered by effort to boost system's capacity," *The Washington Post* (November 28, 2020), https://www.washingtonpost.com/technology/2020/11 /28/amazon-outage-explained/

27 Paris Marx, *Road to Nowhere: What Silicon Valley Gets Wrong about the Future of Transportation* (London: Verso, 2022), 71.

28 Ibid., 72–73.

29 Alice Morby, "Jaguar electrifies its classic E-type car," *Dezeen* (September 8, 2017), https://www.dezeen.com /2017/09/08/jaguar-electrifies-classic-e-type-car-design -transport/

Chapter 3: Trapped In The Present

1 Liam Davenport, "When a Cyberattack Halts Radiation Therapy: Not 'If' but 'When'," Medscape (November 10, 2022), https://www.medscape.com/vie warticle/983847

2 John Scalzi, *Redshirts* (New York: Tor Books, 2012), 35.

3 Ibid., 95.

4 Ibid., 68.

5 Ibid., 64.

6 Gilles Deleuze, *Negotiations: 1972-1990*, trans. Martin Joughin (New York: Columbia University Press, 1995), 129.

7 Yōko Ogawa, *The Memory Police*, trans. Stephen Snyder (New York: Pantheon Books, 2019), 3.
8 Ibid., 135.
9 Ibid., 119.
10 Ibid., 146.
11 Ibid., 158.
12 François J. Bonnet, *After Death*, trans. Amy Ireland and Robin Mackay (Falmouth, UK: Urbanomic, 2020), 28.
13 Ibid., 29.
14 *Cowboy Bebop*, "Speak Like a Child" (English dub), Adult Swim (English air date: October 29, 2001).
15 Liam Stack, "Update Complete: U.S. Nuclear Weapons No Longer Need Floppy Disks," *The New York Times* (October 24, 2019), https://www.nytimes.com/2019/10/24/us/nuclear-weapons-floppy-disks.html
16 Quoted in Gita Jackson, "Why Does Everyone In Netflix's Cowboy Bebop Talk Like That?" *Vice* (November 23, 2021), https://www.vice.com/en/article/v7deax/why-does-everyone-in-netflixs-cowboy-bebop-talk-like-that

Chapter 4: Now And Forever

1 Jim Hougan, *Decadence: Radical Nostalgia, Narcissism, and Decline in the Seventies* (William Morrow and Company, 1975), 194.
2 Ibid.
3 Ibid., 195.
4 Ibid.

5 "Individual Training: Defense Against Enemy Propaganda," Department of the Army, Washington, D.C. (September 15, 1954), 9.

6 "Military Propaganda," Psychological Warfare School, Fort Bragg, North Carolina (February 1953), 24–25.

7 George W. Ball, "The Dangers of Nostalgia," The Department of State, Washington, D.C. (March 1965).

8 Bonnet, *After Death*, 60–61.

9 Ibid., 30.

10 Ibid., 63.

11 Herman Melville, *Moby-Dick or, The Whale* (1851; reissued Penguin Books, 2003), 198.

12 AWS Events, "Amazon re:MARS 2022 – Day 2 – Keynote," YouTube video, 1:54:22 (June 22, 2022), https://www.youtube.com/watch?v=22cb24-sGhg&ab_channel=AWSEvents

13 Roth, "Dying of the Past," 18.

14 Alexander R. Martin, "Nostalgia," *The American Journal of Psychoanalysis*, vol. 14 (1954): 93–104.

15 Ralph Harper, *Nostalgia: An Existential Exploration of Longing and Fulfilment in the Modern Age* (Cleveland, OH: The Press of Western Reserve University, 1966), 29.

16 Ibid., 27.

17 Ron Magid, "An Expanded Universe," *American Cinematographer*, vol. 78, no. 2 (February 1997).

18 Ibid.

19 Alexandra Alter and Elizabeth A. Harris, "As Classic Novels Get Revised for Today's Readers, a Debate About Where to Draw the Line," *The New York Times* (April 5, 2023), https://www.nytimes.com/2023/04/03

/books/classic-novels-revisions-agatha-christie-roald
-dahl.html

20 "Nowism: Why Currency Is the New Currency,"
TrendWatching (2009), https://www.trendwatching
.com/trends/nowism

21 Ibid.

22 Ibid.

POLITY END USER LICENSE AGREEMENT
Go to http://politybooks.com/eula/ to access Polity's ebook EULA.